MW01518561

MOON SHOT

Hypersonic Business Growth Strategies
for Culture, Marketing & Operations

JAMES PHILIP **ARBUCKLE**

KANE **CARPENTER**

CONTENTS

ABOUT THE AUTHORS

James Philip Arbuckle

James Philip Arbuckle is a serial entrepreneur, startup investor, philanthropist, music producer, and business thought leader who has built several multimillion-dollar businesses over the past two decades. He is the founder and chairman of Heavy Hitter Holdings.

However, James is no ordinary entrepreneur. Raised in a working-class neighborhood in Downriver, Michigan, James grew up with a natural street hustle and an aggressive outlook on business and life.

James's ambition led him, while still in his teens, to start several companies selling a variety of goods. An avid reader, James spent hours and hours in the local bookstore, flipping through manual after manual and textbook after textbook. Through these books, James explored a world far wider than his Downriver roots. Ever ambitious, James became one of the youngest recipients of the Microsoft Certified Systems Engineer (MCSE) certification in the state of Michigan. This achievement served as the launchpad for a successful career in technology. Today, James's holdings organization, Heavy Hitter Holdings, is home to more than a dozen brands spanning recruiting and executive search, market research, human capital consulting, digital marketing, CPG products, music, digital media and publishing, and startup investing. Through his YouTube and social media channels, James's ideas reach hundreds of thousands weekly. To learn more about James and his latest projects, visit jamesphilip.com and follow him on Instagram: @jamesphilip313.

Kane Carpenter

Kane Carpenter is a marketer, a growth consultant, and the managing director at Daggerfinn, a boutique employer branding, growth strategies, and organizational development consultancy, where his practice has helped drive substantial growth for some of the most well-known professional services and consumer staples brands around. Daggerfinn lives at the intersection of marketing, workplace culture, and technology, providing business leaders with strategies, tactics, insights, and tools to unlock new levels of growth for their corporations.

Kane is also a *Forbes* contributor, serves as the host of the *Marketing Unlocked* series on Careerology, and shares his thoughts on marketing and finance through his Substack, *No Brand Left Behind*. His articles and videos, published through his Kane at Daggerfinn YouTube channel, reach thousands weekly. He holds an MBA from the Chicago Booth School of Business. To read more of Kane's work, visit kanecarpenter.com or connect with him on Twitter: @kanedcarpenter.

MOON SHOT

Hypersonic Business Growth Strategies
for Culture, Marketing & Operations

JAMES PHILIP **ARBUCKLE**

KANE **CARPENTER**

Published by Allentown Publishing

First Edition: October 2023

ISBN 13: 979-8-9889097-6-7

ISBN 13: 979-8-9889097-5-0

Library of Congress Control Number: 2023914708

Printed in the United States of America

INTRODUCTION

This book is going to break away from the typical business book you've encountered before. Our aim is to present a unique dual perspective on each topic, representing our individual viewpoints based on our own experience and expertise, throughout this book.

As such, you'll find that each chapter is broken down into two perspectives: James's perspective on the subject and Kane's. At times, you'll find that our commentary has a candid and entertaining quality, peppered with pop culture references for a touch of edutainment. On other occasions, our views are more analytical and insight-driven.

Our objective while writing was to craft a book you'd eagerly read from cover to cover while walking away with some ideas and the motivation to make great things happen. We are two people who are completely different in almost every way, shape, and form, but when it comes to business, we think very much alike. We've been a powerful combination for the companies we've built and for the clients we've advised, acting more as growth hackers than traditional management consultants. Think of us as your business consiglieres, your behind-the-scenes shadow board, or, even occasionally, your devil's advocates.

We've journeyed through the thick and thin of business and earned our battle scars. To put it humorously, we've "been there, done that, got the T-shirt, sold it, and then started a T-shirt company." That was a joke, but we indeed ventured into an apparel business a few years ago.

Our focus in this book is centered on three key areas that commonly emerge in our companies and those of our clients: human capital and culture, marketing for growth, and operations. Under the umbrella of culture, we discuss employer branding, nurturing an internal culture, hiring wisely, and dismissing unfit matches. Dealing with human capital and culture over the past decade has become, arguably, the most difficult aspect of running a company. And in this post-COVID world, it continues to get even more complicated. It's just not easy to employ people anymore.

We are both very creative people and live for marketing and advertising. When pushing growth, you often lean on the marketing team, but when that doesn't suffice, we help clients build effective sales teams and strategies as part of comprehensive business process engineering. There is nothing quite like having your marketing team humming and a sales force that's out there closing the leads as they're coming in. We'll cover topics from social media marketing to our theory on monolithic marketing and how this all integrates with employer branding.

Rest assured that operations has certainly not been overlooked. Operations used to be the hardest part of running a business, but we'd argue that in today's world, it's dealing with people. On the operations side, we talk about strategy, customer service, and even cash flow. After all, who the hell doesn't suffer from cash flow problems with bums out there not paying their bills?

Many of our insights will sound off the cuff. But this is exactly how it sounds when we're in the boardroom together. We're not pulling any punches, we're not self-censoring, and, in an aggressive manner, we're not worried about emotions and feelings. We're focused on results. Or, as we often talk about, we're looking for yield. We're always trying to find that spot on the chart where the smallest input generates the maximum output. That's efficiency. There is no other way to live in today's business climate. The ground is shifting beneath our feet, technology and AI are changing everything around us, and the world has never been more competitive. So we see no choice other than to be bold and strategic if we plan to grow at the rates we want to. This is the same mentality we have when we work on consulting products for clients.

Admittedly, we're not cheap, but we are confident that when we work on a consulting project, our clients are going to back up the Brinks truck full of cash. Our clients pay for our solutions to solve their problems and achieve their desired results. We've always known people aren't paying us just to tell them things they want to hear.

That unfaltering philosophy extends to this book. We know we might sell more copies if we tell everyone the things they want to hear, but that's just not how we roll. We wrote this book to tell you the things you *need* to hear so you can take the necessary actions to achieve your business goals. Now that the rules of engagement have been set, turn the page and let's start this journey of growth together.

SECTION ONE
CULTURE

1

EMPLOYER
BRANDING DECEPTION

James's Candid Perspective

We have a big one on the line! The human resources manager straps the hiring manager into the fighting chair on the back of a Viking Sportfish. Then the hiring manager reels and reels and tries to land it. But once they get it in the boat, the fish finds a way to flop itself out, right back into the water, never to be seen again.

This is a systematic issue across the Fortune 1000s at the moment, and it has spread to nearly all companies, regardless of size and industry. Let's call it "industrial-scale catfishing." Companies often catfish potential employees, both unintentionally and intentionally, when trying to appeal to the market forces of what is in style at the moment. This is similar to what happens on dating sites, for example, especially now with dating apps working in full force. You see someone with good photos, you have chatted with them for weeks or sometimes even months as "schedules always conflict," and then the big day comes—you meet them! You walk into the bar and right past them. Why? Because they look nothing like their profile photo. Then, as you talk to them in real time, you find out they are not as crafty and witty without having a day to come up with a clever response to your question.

You're disappointed, but you try to be a champ and stick it out for a drink or two because you want to give it an honest try. In the end, it's just not a fit. You shake hands or give one of those "I kind of don't want to touch you" half-assed one-armed hugs and walk out the door just to instantly start swiping away.

That's basically how it goes in the corporate world. A new employee starts and instantly finds out the company isn't as cute as its profile pic. They give it an honest go, then, after a couple of months, they decide to leave as it's not what they were expecting.

There is one caveat to this—prospective employees often hear one thing and process it as another. A company will say it has a merit-based vacation policy under which performance will dictate how much or how often employees can take time off beyond sick days. The new employee hears "unlimited vacation time," and when they can't take a month off in their first six months while also underperforming, they quit and go on Glassdoor to say the company has deceptive hiring practices.

The social media accounts of some major companies paint an image of work-life balance. In reality, in order to stay on top of their industry, their employees have to put in hard work and sometimes long hours. Don't paint a portrait of being on vacation all the time and having brunch at 11:00 a.m. on Friday after a 9:00 a.m. in-office yoga class. Employees will more than likely be in meetings or on calls with customers for most of the day on Friday.

What type of people are you, as a hiring manager, attracting with this approach? Do you want people who are focused on working less or people who want to help grow the business and concentrate on the mission of the company? What is the lesson here? Don't fake the funk just to get people on the dance floor. You'll end up looking like an overserved wedding guest at 2:00 a.m. Stop worrying about having the kegerator, the Ping-Pong tables, and unlimited vacation policies unless that is what you're about and that is the kind of employee you want to attract.

It's okay to say, "We work hard here. This is where you come to build a career, and we work hard and play harder." Give examples. "You may work a lot of hours Monday through Thursday, then leave at 2:00 p.m. on Friday." Be honest about the work environment and the culture. If you keep trying to appeal to people who want to do anything but work, don't be surprised when they show up and don't want to work.

The cost of distraction is second only to the cost of turnover. Your public employer branding and interview process should resemble the real culture of the company. If you need to sprinkle in some extra toppings, like you're ordering a Cold Stone waffle bowl, to sweeten the deal, then do it, but never stray from your company's brand image.

Kane's Considered Viewpoint

There has been a seismic shift in the way companies market themselves as employers over the past decade, with a trend toward uppity and unrealistic self-promotion accelerating over the past handful of years. Where once companies hung their reputations on hard work, long hours, and a get-things-done-at-all-costs attitude, today's companies are increasingly portraying themselves as places where work comes second to wellness—both mental and physical—awareness of social issues, virtue signaling, and the ability to bring "your whole self to work." In order to attract younger talent that is leaving school more and more disillusioned with capitalism, companies are changing their employer brands and employer value propositions (EVPs).

Regardless of what you think of this societal shift toward work-life balance being front and center of nearly every conversation around employment, there are externalities that we, as marketers, need to be aware of. And with any externality, there is an opportunity to capitalize and out-market the competition. Here's the issue that needs to be solved over the next few years: do companies, which intrinsically are places where we complete work so we can support our families and personal lives, continue to present false fronts of overwhelming work-life balance (of employees sitting on beaches every Tuesday and doing spin classes together on Thursday midmornings) at the risk of subjecting themselves to adverse selection?

Adverse selection is an idea, widely used in economic theory, that explains what happens when one side of an interaction (in this case, workers) has more information than the other (the company). For example, by advertising themselves as carefree, workless places of employment (with the idea of attracting better employees who are pursuing reasonable work-life balance), are companies attracting workers who don't want to work at all, but who put on a false front during interviews and the hiring process?

Having pondered this problem a lot over the past few years, I think companies are making a mistake with their employer branding when they lean too far into portraying themselves as too life-skewed on the work-life balance scale. In my experience, the best employees enjoy working. Now, this doesn't mean we have to take things to extremes. The best employees like what they do, are efficient and effective, and work when work has to be done. There's no deception because the work ethic is there. If clients need to be serviced, the best employees will step up—no matter the time of day or day of the week. Companies are better off when they position themselves to attract this kind of workers—and, again in my experience, these employees aren't fussed about having every flavor of sustainable sparkling water in the company fridge or whether the complimentary cookies the boss brought in on Friday were made from organic, sustainably sourced ingredients. Work is work, and balance comes in the form of being able to take the necessary time off to take the kids to soccer practice at 3:00 p.m. on a Wednesday because that employee has proven reliable.

Trust is everything when it comes to an effective, collaborative, and supportive work environment. By deploying deceptive employer branding, companies put themselves at risk of bringing on employees who are joining the company under false pretenses and cannot be trusted to do the work when it needs to be done. They're only there for the parts of the work-life balance equation that don't involve work.

2

GANG MENTALITY

James's Aggressive Take

One of my favorite laughs in the office was a few years back. Someone was reading an article about a couple of motorcycle clubs whose members were beating each other up in a Starbucks parking lot with hammers over a turf war or something. While I don't fully remember the exact details of that news report, I found it funny as it's how I think of business. It's how we win at business. We wake up in the morning ready to beat up our competitors with long wood-framing hammers until the block is ours.

Then we go block by block until we have them all. Never was it the plan to wake up in the morning and give up market share. We are always looking to dominate the market, regardless of what business line or sector we are doing battle in that day.

That sounds aggressive, I know, but have you ever witnessed someone staying in business for two decades and also enduring three recessions while going at it soft? You won't find many, so let me save you the trouble of looking. It's the equivalent of having the strength that men can achieve only through forty years of hard work that built forearms of steel. That strength didn't come without calluses. In this day and age, we want buttery soft hands that have never seen a day of real work, yet we still want that strength of steel when we are sixty. It doesn't work that way.

This mentality should come from the top down. Get everyone thinking about strategy and marketing. Get everyone talking about sales. Develop a brute force mindset within your organization that is unstoppable. How do you plan to stay in business, let alone dominate a market, if your workforce doesn't care if you win or lose?

We will use this example often in this book because everyone is dealing with this issue. Companies tend to sink when they have a few people drilling holes in the back of the boat while their leaders try to captain the ship. If you have people on your team who want to sink to the bottom, cut them loose and allow them to float away for the gulls to pick at.

Beyond the culture aspect, you also have to come full force at your competitors. Find every way to dominate them. Make more sales calls, do more social media, get more positive PR, offer more products and services, open earlier and close later, fill the search engines with great content, and so forth. Keep pushing every metric that matters until you make your competitors feel claustrophobic. Make them feel like the walls are caving in and they have nowhere to run.

When you have your whole team thinking this way, your opposition will likely fade away, if not fold altogether. Get everyone on the team rowing in one direction with a level of vigor they don't teach in school anymore. This is the way to rapid growth during times when it seems like people want to do less. It's a battle of attrition as all markets are competitive; you just have to keep grinding until you win the war.

Kane's Approachable Angle

Developing a world-class team is something I think about often. While I used to think the best professional teams were built on foundations that looked almost familial, I've come around to the idea that I was wrong. The best professional teams look and feel more like gangs. At the end of the day, gangs are more cutthroat, more fearsome, and more effective than families at getting things done.

Why have I come around to this idea? Because the best teams need to be solely focused on one objective. Families are notorious for being distracted. Hell, just think about the last family gathering you were at and how disjointed the conversations were. Gangs, on the other hand, are ruthlessly efficient. Don't agree with the direction? You're gone.

But that's enough of my amateur armchair-family-versus-gang analysis. What's the takeaway for small businesses operating in an increasingly competitive environment? It is the importance of aligning your core team members, especially in the early days of the business, to one mission. Building a business is challenging, to say the least, and you need a team of talented individuals all rowing in the same direction in order to generate any momentum—even then, success is not guaranteed.

I remember a case study I read at business school that looked at the importance of an entrepreneur's vision and sales execution in the beginning stages of getting a startup off the ground. When running a small business, you need to be responsive to market dynamics—to be able to iterate your product or service or delivery or a host of other variables at the drop of a hat. You need to be capable of raising and dropping your prices, and your sales team also needs to learn to adapt quickly. As the captain of your ship, you need to be able to tell your crew to jump, and their response needs to be "How high?"

Without a core team that showcases this level of adaptability and dedication to getting things right at your small business, you're rowing against the tide. This is why you need to build your gang and imbue it with this mentality of strength. You need to ensure you give the business the best possible chance of succeeding. Remember, something like six in seven small businesses will close. Fight with all your might to not be one of those—and do it with your gang members alongside you.

3

WHY YOU NEED AN INNER CIRCLE

James's Honest Outlook

I was once on a flight from DTW to MIA, and as I settled down and waited for the flight attendant to bring me a scotch, I turned on CNBC. The reporters were talking about United Airlines coming to terms with contracts that would increase pilots' pay by up to 40 percent or something.

I fired off a text to a group chat Kane is a part of. "Well, it looks like wage inflation shows no signs of slowing."

Kane's response was: "I like my pilots well compensated."

That made for a nice preflight laugh, but over the next couple of hours, I had to think about it. Kane's quip reflected what is happening in real time for anyone in a leadership role after COVID. Your inner circle—whether that is people you can't afford to lose or people who have little room for error—likely have to be well compensated, perhaps even overcompensated at times. They add the most value and they are the most difficult to recruit. The real truth is, when you lose these people, it just plain hurts.

Airlines have learned to operate in this manner. Who can't you live without? Well, you need pilots who show up, are reliable, and don't crash into shit. You also need highly skilled people who maintain the jets, which allows them to fly safely and on time. These are the people you don't want to lose to high turnover, which represents about 20 percent of your staff. Then there is the remaining 80 percent. These people may be those at the ticket counter, flight attendants, ground crew, customer service, and even janitors. These roles typically have high turnover anyway, but often have the highest candidate flow as well. They are also all critical roles, but slightly easier ones to deal with if you have a turnover issue. I like my maintenance crew well compensated too.

In an ideal world, you would create a culture where you're trying to retain good employees regardless of what titles they hold. But when you have a budget to maintain, that isn't always the case. We now have a new problem. As the workforce and attitudes toward work change, everyone is fighting for that top 20 percent. Wait a year and that may be reduced to 15 percent. So, if you're operating in a world with perpetual worker shortages and highly skilled or sought-after workers are in great demand, you better batten down the hatches.

This means to make sure your compensation is on point and keeping up as wage inflation skyrockets. Are your work environment and benefits competitive? Do these key stakeholders feel valued and a part of the company? How will you replace them if your employer brand is weak?

There was a time when companies viewed employees as expendable, and that was the wrong way to think. We always hear people say that "everyone is replaceable," which is true, until it isn't. As every single day goes by, it is becoming increasingly difficult to find good people, let alone employ them.

I agree with Kane. I like my doctors, lawyers, and pilots well compensated. Use that same mindset when it comes to your key employees, whether they are your president, sales associates, or engineers. List those employees you cannot afford to lose and do everything you can to keep them. In a world where loyalty has gone out the window and job-hopping is now cool, make sure you have a recruitment strategy to deal with the high turnover of the other 80 percent. It doesn't get any easier from here, so plan accordingly.

Kane's Textbook Viewpoint

Picture the best and most efficient teams you've ever seen, those winning organizations that seem to have an unspoken understanding, operating as one cohesive unit, executing flawlessly. Or envision a high-powered individual, seemingly imbued with uncanny wisdom and clarity of thought, navigating the maze of life and business with an unerring instinct for the right course. In both scenarios, at the core of success, you'll discover the secret weapon: the inner circle.

Understanding the concept of the inner circle requires the ability to view it through two distinctive lenses. The first focuses on a core team of employees around which the rest of your enterprise revolves. The second expands this concept beyond your organization, capturing a select group of like-minded individuals who inspire, motivate, and guide you.

Let's delve into the first interpretation—your business's core team. Think of its members as the beating heart of your business operations, the people you trust implicitly with the direction and growth of your company. James once imparted a valuable lesson that has held true for years: "Your team is your first product." Indeed the skill, dedication, and culture of this inner circle set the tone for your company's overall performance. They are the fulcrum upon which your organization pivots. The inner circle isn't just about a group of top performers. Rather, it's about identifying those individuals who not only excel in their roles but also embody your company's values, drive its vision, and contribute to a culture of success. The secret to scaling your business effectively lies in building around this core group, entrusting it to make key decisions and empowering it to nurture the rest of the organization.

Now, let's shift our gaze to the second interpretation—your external inner circle. This group is made up of people outside your immediate business environment who bring unique perspectives, challenge your thinking, and provide candid advice. Think of them as your personal board of advisors.

In my journey, the wisdom of my external inner circle has proven an invaluable resource. Just like an eagle uses the winds to soar, successful entrepreneurs harness the collective wisdom of their external inner circle to elevate their vision and perspective. This is a diverse assembly of experienced entrepreneurs, mentors, and peers who can provide insights into different industries, challenge your assumptions, and share lessons from their own triumphs and failures. A thriving external inner circle is not about surrounding yourself with "yes" people but fostering a dynamic collective that enriches your thinking and broadens your horizons. Their advice and guidance can help you avoid pitfalls, navigate challenging decisions, and stay focused on your goals.

While it may seem complex, nurturing both internal and external inner circles is a strategy worth pursuing. It takes a balance of trust, transparency, and continuous learning to sustain these circles. But once you've got them, you're not operating as a lone entrepreneur or business. You've got a strong core of individuals propelling your company from within and a wise counsel of advisors steering you from without. The inner circle is more than just a clique or a group. It is a strategic alliance that helps drive your business forward and ensures you're never alone on your entrepreneurial journey. It is your sounding board, your source of strength and inspiration, your safety net, and your guiding star, propelling you to make the right moves and reach for the stars. That is why you need an inner circle.

4

WRONG PERSON, WRONG SEAT

Kane's Pragmatic Perspective

There's a dangerous phenomenon that can creep into businesses of all sizes and types, eating away at productivity, impacting efficiency, and perhaps most destructively, wreaking havoc on organizational culture. It's a problem that is as pervasive as it is under-recognized: the issue of the wrong person in the wrong position.

Let's start with an analogy to illustrate the point. Picture a world-class sprinter, trained and conditioned for maximum speed over short distances. Now imagine placing that same sprinter in a marathon, a race requiring endurance, pacing, and a vastly different set of skills. It's not that the sprinter lacks talent or ability; they're simply not suited for this particular race. The outcome? Inefficiency, frustration, and likely failure to finish the race.

Now apply this to a business context. An employee may be exceptionally talented in their field, but if their skills and style don't align with their role, the results can be just as disastrous. When the wrong person is in the wrong position, productivity dips. The employee may struggle to perform tasks that don't play to their strengths or interests. Deadlines may be missed, projects delayed, and overall output diminished. Not only does this directly affect the bottom line, but it also impacts morale and motivation.

Efficiency falls, too. Tasks take longer to complete when someone isn't equipped with the right skills or mindset for the job. Resources are squandered, time is wasted, and the knock-on effects ripple throughout the business. The wrong person in the wrong position can also lead to increased errors, requiring time-consuming and costly corrections.

The implications for the company's culture are perhaps the most profound. When an individual is struggling or feeling misplaced, it breeds dissatisfaction and negativity. This can be incredibly infectious within a team and can quickly erode a previously positive work culture.

Having the wrong person in the wrong position also undermines trust in leadership. It raises questions about the decision-making process, competence, and overall judgment of the people at the helm. If left unaddressed, this trust deficit can evolve into a serious threat to the stability and future success of the business. So, how to tackle this? How can you ensure you're not placing a square peg into a round hole?

The first step is cultivating a deep understanding of the skills, abilities, and preferences of each team member. This comes from effective communication, comprehensive job profiling, and a variety of assessment tools.

It also comes from creating an environment where employees feel safe to express their aspirations, interests, and concerns.

Next, when filling a position, resist the temptation to simply slot in an available person. Instead, match the specific demands of the role with the abilities and aspirations of the candidate. Sometimes, this might mean leaving a role vacant a little longer until the right match is found, or investing in training and development to equip an existing team member with the necessary skills.

It's also vital to be vigilant and responsive. Regular performance reviews, feedback sessions, and open dialogue can help identify when someone is struggling or feeling misplaced. If you do find a misalignment, don't be afraid to make changes. Reassign roles, alter job descriptions, or consider lateral moves to better match your people with positions that play to their strengths. Remember having the wrong person in the wrong position is a lose-lose situation: the individual feels frustrated and unfulfilled and the business suffers. By ensuring the right fit between individuals and roles, you can create a win-win situation: a fulfilling work environment for your employees and a thriving, efficient, and positive business culture.

James's Shrewd Assessment

If you want to be a successful leader, whether that's running your own department or if you're at the helm of your own company or someone else's, you must understand the right fit. Often as leaders we come across incandescently brilliant people, yet we watch them struggle and sometimes we can't figure out why. This person is a mental giant but just can't seem to buy themselves a win in this role. At other times, people lack the capability and they're in the wrong role, all at the same damn time.

The art of this is figuring out where to put people who are really good at something. If you don't have a role for them, make one. You need to keep these people on your team. Everyone is out there fighting for that top 10 or 20 percent of talent. If you have someone who is in the top 5 percent of talent, don't let them go. If you don't have space for them, make some. You must find a place where they can excel. At times, you will have to coach somebody and help them discover a new path in life, likely with a different company because you can't find a seat for them to succeed in at yours.

This is what we call matching and mismatching. You see this all the time in large corporations. Theoretically, you see more mismatching than matching. These companies hire the best people with the highest GPAs from the best colleges, yet they put them in a seat in which they just can't thrive. These people can add a tremendous amount of value to their company if they can just get to the right position in the right department. But, as in most large companies, politics and red tape often hold these people back from doing their best work.

Then you have the other issue where you have the wrong person in the wrong seat—what we call a bad hire. There's no sense in moving this person around from seat to seat trying to find the right fit. Many hiring managers in corporate America don't like to admit they made a mistake. We often talk about that old saying "slow to hire, fast to fire." If you know they're the wrong fit either by ability or culturally, hanging on to them does everyone a disservice. But what do you need to figure out whether it is the right person in the wrong seat or the wrong person for the company?

Always give people a chance—it's only fair. If they keep making massive screwups or their performance on the job indicates they don't care, that's reason enough to part ways. If an employee is honestly trying to do better, morally and ethically, it's a good idea to give them a chance.

Many companies suffer from all of this. They have the right people in the wrong seats. They have the wrong people in the right seats. Let's digest that for a minute: the wrong people in the right seats. This is one of those cases where technically, based on experience and job title, this is where they're supposed to be. They're just not doing a good job. This is a scenario where you can coach up or coach out, but you can't let them drag the company down. We talk a lot about the inner circle and trying to keep your best employees. Part of that is making sure you have the right people in the right seats and you're facilitating an environment that allows them to thrive.

One of the greatest things we learned while doing workforce consulting and culture development is that people are encouraged to do what they love and what they had a passion for as children. No one told them how unsatisfied people are with their lives if they're doing what they love but they're terrible at it. People in general get great satisfaction when they do a good job, regardless of what that job is. Keep in mind when you're trying to make a talent fit that the right person in the right seat makes the most sense when the individual thrives fulfilling that function. As they receive the dopamine hit from the satisfaction of doing the job well, they will only continue to get better at it.

5

HIRE THE RIGHT ONES, FIRE THE QUESTIONABLE

James's Assertive Position

There is no way to put it nicely or kindly. One of the most common sayings amongst the C-Suite is: "slow to hire, fast to fire." Sure, it rhymes, but not the happy kind of rhyme your kids sing. If they do sing it, you're raising complete savages who will have high chances of becoming billionaires, so keep up the solid parenting!

You learn over the years that hiring the right people is much like dating. If you're doing it right, you have gone on a lot of first dates. Maybe you have been slapped or even had a drink thrown in your face, but, sooner or later, you find the right match. In highly competitive markets, you're left searching for diamonds in the rough, so this process takes even more time.

One lesson you learn sooner or later is one you wish you hadn't had to learn in the first place. We all remember that lesson far too well. You had a great first interview, maybe got a little emotional or thought your gut instinct was right, and you made a fast hire.

Oh, damn, you still remember that one, don't you? Oh, no. Did you do it a second time? There's nothing wrong with moving swiftly, but don't get emotional. Don't cut your due diligence short. Follow the process to the end.

The "slow to hire" part is essentially interviewing a pool of candidates in order to gauge the market. The second part is putting the final candidates through well-thought-out and planned interviews so you can make the best hire. You can do all that and still make the wrong hire. Well, back to swiping all day until you find another match.

The "fast to fire" part sounds bad, but it's not. You're not saying, "Draw and quarter them until they quit!" It comes down to this: when the wrong person is in the wrong role, you are doing everyone a disservice by letting them continue to fail. Another risk—especially when they are very negative—is that they can poison the people around them, which can cause you to lose more people.

If you have been in business long enough, you've noticed that frequently, it is not only one person who leaves. Two or three people in the same clique will often leave over a two-month period. That's because the well was poisoned and allowing these negative people more time to spread their cancer costs you even more employees. It's one thing if they lack the ability to do the job and you're giving them a chance. But if they themselves are the so-called toxic environment they speak of, you can't allow them to ruin your entire culture.

It is a new world out there. Every year that goes by, it becomes more difficult to employ the younger generations. You can work around generational shifts, but, as stated earlier, you can't work around people who keep drilling holes in the ship while you're trying to captain it.

Kane's Prescriptive Approach

When navigating the challenging terrain of running a small business, the team you choose to accompany you on your journey is crucial. But it's not just about gathering warm bodies to fill up office chairs. It's about finding the right talent—individuals who not only possess the necessary skills, but are also a good fit for your company's culture and values. Equally, it's about having the courage to let go of those who are not serving your business's mission.

For a hiring manager at a small business, it's easy to fall into the trap of thinking the talent pool is shallow, that it's not as abundant as the one larger organizations swim in. But the truth is, talent is everywhere—it's finding the right people and knowing when to part ways with the questionable ones that is the real challenge.

When it comes to hiring, don't just focus on the skills listed on a résumé. Dig deeper. Is this person a cultural fit? Do their values align with those of your company? Are they adaptable, able to wear multiple hats, as is often required in a small business setting? Hire individuals who not only possess the skills your business needs, but also demonstrate a passion for their work and a drive to grow—the "right ones" who will contribute significantly to your business.

Once you've brought the right people on board, invest in their growth. Remember your employees are not cogs in a machine; they're human beings with aspirations. Promote a culture of continuous learning and professional development. Encourage creativity and innovation. This will not only benefit your business, but also foster an environment that attracts and retains top talent.

On the flip side, when you encounter individuals who aren't pulling their weight or who are causing more harm than good, make the tough decision—let them go. It's not an easy decision, and it's one many small business owners grapple with, but it's an essential part of ensuring the health of your business. The reality is that every person on a small team makes a significant impact. Underperformers or individuals who aren't aligned with your company's culture can quickly drain your financial and emotional resources. The longer you delay addressing these issues, the more damage they do to your team's morale and your bottom line.

"Firing fast" is not about being heartless. It's about recognizing that in the fast-paced, high-stakes world of small business, every decision counts and every team member plays a critical role. It's about understanding that allowing underperformance to persist sends a message to your other employees that mediocrity is tolerated, which can be detrimental to your overall company culture.

Navigating the talent pool can indeed be a challenging endeavor for hiring managers of small businesses. However, by being strategic and steadfast in your hiring practices and brave in your decisions to part ways, you're setting your business up for success. In the end, the golden rule is simple: hire slow, hire smart, and, when needed, fire fast. Your company's success depends on the collective strength, skill, and commitment of your team. It's worth taking the time to find the right people, and it's crucial to have the courage to let those go who don't fit the bill. Remember every person on your team counts—make sure they're the right ones.

6

YOU CAN'T HAVE *CULTURE* WITHOUT *CULT*

Kane's Considered Point of View

A healthy company culture is more than a pleasant workplace environment. It's the glue that holds together the shared beliefs and values of the entire organization. The power of this phenomenon lies in a word tucked away within the word *culture*: *cult*. Now, don't jump to conclusions; this isn't about forming a rigid sect or espousing dogmatic beliefs. *Cult* here signifies a group of individuals bound by a common purpose—creating a positive force in the corporate world.

Let's start from the inside: the nucleus of the organization. This consists of the core team members who first subscribed to the company's vision, embodying the company's ethos in their actions and decisions. They're the torchbearers of the company culture, setting the tone for the entire organization.

The online shoe and clothing retailer Zappos serves as an example. The company has prioritized creating an energetic, customer-focused culture. This has resulted in a reputation for extraordinary customer service that has distinguished Zappos in the competitive e-commerce market. Similarly, the outdoor clothing brand Patagonia has woven its commitment to environmental conservation into its corporate culture. This shared passion among the employees has drawn in customers who identify with the company's ethos and helped solidify Patagonia's unique brand identity.

So how do you cultivate this magnetic force within your own business? The journey begins with the hiring process. Skills and experience are important, but finding employees with whom the company's mission and values resonate is the true key to a strong culture.

Once the right people are on board, it's important to immerse them in the company's culture immediately. Orientation sessions, mentorship programs, and frequent interactions with the core team can help new hires understand and adapt to the company culture. Encouraging open dialogue can create an environment where everyone feels included and valued, which strengthens the sense of community.

Acknowledging and rewarding employees who reflect the company's values is another crucial step. This not only motivates them, but it also sets an example for other employees. Finally, investing in the development of these cultural pillars can lead to the formation of future leaders who will carry the company's values forward as it grows.

The ultimate goal is not to create a uniform mass, but to gather a team of diverse individuals unified in their belief in the company's mission. The strength of your company's culture lies in these individuals. They are the embodiment of the company's values and the inspiration for their colleagues. In essence, building a robust culture necessitates a dash of *cult*.

James's Insightful Standpoint

Franklin Covey used to display motivational posters inside its stores. If you don't know what those were, it wouldn't be hard to figure out your age. These posters featured sayings like "There is no I in team" and the accompanying photo would depict something like a single waterdrop in a puddle full of ripples—the type of thing that really didn't motivate anyone. Perhaps you're thinking that sounds pretty goddamn corny. What you didn't see at that store was a poster saying that "You can't have *culture* without *cult*."

I can only imagine what the hell that poster would look like. It makes me wonder if I jumped into some graphics-based AI portal right now and asked it to create that picture, would it show me a place like Waco, Texas, or a bunch of people wearing matching shoes? But that's not the kind of cult we're talking about here. In a good culture, everyone believes in the shared vision and operates in similar ways, all while trying to reach a common goal.

As we typically say, it's really hard to run a business if people are in the back of the boat drilling holes while you're trying to captain the ship. Even if that happens because of one bad actor, if you have the right culture, your team will pick up buckets and start bailing. In a bad culture, people drill holes or simply watch as the ship sinks.

We talk about the post-COVID work environment a lot as many of our customers are struggling with this workforce fog that hasn't lifted. It's probably the most difficult time in history to build a good corporate culture when everyone wants to work from home while also not caring about the company itself. If you're lucky, you have that inner core that truly believes in the culture and the company. They care about where it's going, and you hope it trickles down to everybody else.

But hope isn't a plan. In an ideal world, you hire people who not only can function in the job, but also fit the culture. When everyone is rowing in the same direction, things are certainly easier. If you have a culture of always striving for excellence but you hire people who have a "that's good enough" attitude, those hires don't make for a good work environment for anybody. Some of the fastest-growing and greatest companies in the world got there because they had a group of people who had a similar operational tempo and common goals.

No company on the planet has all of its people perfectly aligned. Some employees believe a job is work; you show up to work and you go home. They're never going to be personally invested in the culture of the company. If you manage people like this, that is actually not a bad spot to be in. You are surrounded by capable people who can get the job done well and on time. You really can't ask for much more than that.

In a weird way, many companies are like brackish water where freshwater and saltwater meet. Some employees bleed the company colors and are very loyal while others believe it is a place to earn a paycheck and then go home. They all blend, and it works. Sometimes, if you're lucky, you can drag the worker bee types into the culture. Other times, it's not worth the effort. Maybe it's best to leave people alone and let them get their work done.

The people you have to watch out for are the anti-culture types. These typically are not people who show up, do their jobs, and go home, and who have nothing bad to say about anybody. These are typically people who gossip behind everyone's backs, spreading rumors and lies, who are also constantly negative. They're not just anti-culture; they're poisonous. They tend to ruin every work environment they enter. No one likes working with these people. They drag everyone down and make no attempt to lift anybody up.

Most competitive companies build a cultural framework around hard work, high levels of customer service, innovation, and teamwork. These all are good things to strive for in any company. Encountering a negative, anti-culture employee must be a "fast fire" moment. There should be no tolerance for them at the end of the day. You don't have to drink the Kool-Aid, but you can't go around throwing it in people's faces either.

If you're an employee at Toyota and Lexus, for example, striving for excellence and quality across the organization is tantamount, whereas a company such as Four Seasons prioritizes the highest levels of customer service across every touch point that guests will ever experience. When you start a business, you spend a lot of time focusing on the company mission statement, but how much time do you spend developing a company manifesto or culture plan? Modern-day consulting has a lot of companies concentrating on EVPs, which every company should have, but why not have some simple words around what your culture is?

This could be something as simple as a tag cloud like you see on blogs. Some larger words in size and some smaller words based on level of importance is one way to do this. Words like *excellence* or *quality* or *customer service* or *innovation* to things like creativity or kindness or mindfulness. It's okay to set expectations for culture just as you would for performance. Do you really want to employ someone who is constantly talking behind everyone else's back and creating widespread distrust? You'll probably find out most people don't want to employ that person nor does anyone want to work beside them.

What about a culture of mutual respect even if you disagree? Is that even possible in today's world? You certainly won't know if you don't try.

We won't sit here and act like we're sports experts, but we have studied sports teams quite diligently over the years in terms of teamwork and achieving high goals. You'll read stories about a team that didn't have a roster full of Jordans; maybe they didn't have anyone who was even close to Jordan. They had a bunch of good players but no great players, yet somehow they ended up as champions. When you look at it, you realize they were almost like a cult in the sense of what they believed in and how strongly. They believed they were fully capable of winning and that they were surrounded by people who had their back, which allowed them to develop a camaraderie no one else in the league had.

It's hard to do that now with everyone working from home, so get people back in the office even if it's just a couple of days a week. You can't build camaraderie through a teleconference with a bunch of people who may have never even met before. Gather everyone in an environment where people can laugh and have fun and be themselves. We all face a long road to recovery after what happened in 2020, but you can't give up.

7

CULTURE TRAPS: MAKE WORK ABOUT WORK AGAIN

James's Crafty Outlook

One of the greatest pitfalls in the past ten to fifteen years was tech companies setting workplace trends. How many companies rearranged their office spaces? Do you have an open floor plan like Google's?

In recent years, reports have come out of employees talking about how they absolutely hate the open floor plan. Look at other tech companies. They have Ping-Pong tables and kegerators. Some companies even have nap pods.

My big first tech job was at a headquarters for an automotive company. It had a cafeteria, but you still had to pay for the food. Having a cafeteria or a restaurant within a large building is nothing new, but for some employees of tech companies the food is free. This leaves companies in the manufacturing sector, for example, with their backs against the wall.

People on the shop floor can't take naps and such companies don't have the margin to do all the cool shit.

Companies spent so much time trying to become like other companies that they forgot who they are. You're going to have to do certain things to attract top talent. On the other hand, if you just start doing what everyone else is doing, you're going to lose your identity as well.

We have a slogan at Daggerfinn. We tell clients to "make work about work again." The new generations have a completely different idea of what work should be. When your company creates an environment that supports that, it ends up becoming a deadly cocktail. Many people's idea of work today is not working at all. And we've learned post COVID that people are now of the mindset of doing as little as possible. From minimum Mondays to quiet quitting, it's a constant battle to get people to do the work they're paid for.

See, when you're selling a candidate on the fact that you have nap pods and Ping-Pong tables and kegerators, even massages at your desk and unlimited vacation time, where do you think their mind goes? Nowhere in this equation are you selling the actual work or detailing the contributions they have to make to keep their seat. Six months in, the managers are complaining that all the new hire wants to do is drink beer, play Ping-Pong, and take naps. What the hell did you expect? That's exactly the lifestyle you sold them in the interview.

As I wrote about earlier, we see this same mistake when it comes to employer branding. You'll see it with the Fortune 500s, the new tech unicorns, and the big consulting companies. On Instagram, they'll have a photo of Susie with her husband and child on the beach at 9:00 a.m. on a Tuesday. The caption will say something about work-life balance.

The problem is that's not what 9:00 a.m. on Tuesday looks like—maybe occasionally.

On the flip side of that, we talk a lot about monolithic marketing. It's our concept that everything you do that's outward facing applies to your current and future workforce and also your current and prospective customers. From an employer branding standpoint, the image of Susie on the beach at 9:00 a.m. on a Tuesday might make her more interested in coming to work for you. As a customer, though, all I'm thinking is, "This is why I can't get anyone to answer the damn phone at 9:00 a.m. on a Tuesday." I realize I'm probably going to have poor customer service here and for the egregious amount of money these people are charging, they should be on top of everything, especially in the middle of a workday.

When you talk to clients about this, you often get the deer-in-headlights look because they never even thought of that. It's one thing to cut out early every couple of months in order to take the team out to do something fun. Most customers understand that. If they're constantly having to wait for long periods of time to get their emails answered or their phone calls returned, that isn't good for business. And these problems are all because your culture has turned into an environment where it's playtime every day at 10:00 a.m. You can't be surprised when your customers start going somewhere else that values them.

If you want to stay competitive in the next decade, you're going to have to make work about work and figure out other ways to reward people throughout the year. You're likely better off throwing them a couple of extra vacation days than you are turning the average Monday-through-Friday workweek into a play zone. When you think about it, you can see that only certain industries have this luxury. We have a lot of clients from the manufacturing industry, and they don't have this luxury. Our clients from the hospitality sector don't have it either. Large conglomerates and tech startups do, but that doesn't mean you should model your culture after theirs.

I'm thinking back to a conversation with one of the partners at a law firm I work with. The firm became number one in its state, possibly by now in the entire region. As I've spent so much time in the executive search and recruiting space for the past two decades, I was curious about how the firm attracted so much top talent. I asked what the interview process was like. It came down to this: the firm had a big enough brand image to attract and to actively pursue lawyers from the best law schools.

The pitch reminded me of the movie *Boiler Room*. The character played by Ben Affleck talks about how "you're going to have to work your ass off in this firm." When the hiring managers at this law firm recruited lawyers, they made it more than clear that the job required more than a forty-hour week and if the candidate was going to mentally check out at 4:00 p.m., the firm was not the place for them. They sold the idea of growth, but only growth that comes with hard work. This isn't the place to keep a chair warm.

Sometimes you must be firm and tell people what your culture is. If they don't want to work for you, they don't want to work for you. At times, we bend too much in order to get somebody on board, then six months later, we realize we are better off not having this person at all. Although the world has changed, people still strive for excellence and want to build a career. Maybe they're not going to work fifty or sixty hours a week, but they're going to work really hard during the forty hours they're there because they're not worried about the nap pods and the beer fridge. They want to get somewhere in life.

Another old saying is, if you give people an inch, they will take a mile. And while people are taking that mile, your customers are waiting for phone calls, emails, and other deliverables while half of your team is having a Ping-Pong tournament at 10:37 a.m. on a Thursday. That works for companies like Google that have billions of dollars in cash and margins fatter than the two-pound burrito I just ate, but it may not work so well for you. For the rest of us, these perks are not an option as we're fighting day to day just to stay in business. Take care of your people and reward them well, but don't be afraid to start making work about work again.

Kane's Pragmatic Point of View

In recent years, businesses have been pressured to adopt a work-as-lifestyle approach. This means presenting work not just as a place to make a living, but as a space for self-fulfillment, socialization, and personal growth. In trying to attract top talent, the hiring managers of some companies have embarked on a disingenuous journey of overselling the perks, glossing over the challenges, and painting an unrealistically rosy picture of life at their organizations. It's time to revisit this strategy. It's time to make work about work again.

With the competition for talent increasing, businesses feel compelled to stand out. This has led to an escalating game of one-upmanship, with companies vying to offer the most alluring perks, from in-office massages and pet-friendly policies to fully stocked snack bars and remote work.

However, this can lead to an environment where a glossy veneer obscures the realities of the job, creating mismatched expectations and disillusionment when the sheen wears off.

So how can we make work about work again? The answer lies in authenticity. Authenticity involves communicating the true nature of the job, the work culture, and the organization, warts and all. It's about balancing the highlights with the realities of the day-to-day grind. Adopting this approach has benefits: by providing a clear picture of what the job entails, you attract applicants who are genuinely interested in the role and are prepared to meet its demands. They are likely to be more motivated, productive, and satisfied, leading to reduced turnover and a more harmonious work environment. Honesty and transparency foster trust, which is crucial to employee engagement and loyalty. Trust in leadership has been linked to increased job satisfaction, better performance, and lower stress levels.

The first step in adopting this approach is to conduct an honest evaluation of your organization and the roles you're looking to fill. What are the day-to-day tasks? What challenges will employees face? What is the culture really like?

Once you've established a truthful picture, convey this in your recruitment materials. Rather than focusing on the perks, highlight the substance of the work and its impact. Let applicants know what kind of problems they'll be solving, what projects they'll be working on, and how their role fits into the organization's broader mission.

Last, encourage current employees to share their experiences. This could be through testimonials, videos, or even social media takeovers. This not only gives potential applicants an unfiltered glimpse into life at your organization, but it also boosts the trust and engagement of current employees by giving them a voice.

Let's look at a concrete example: a call center. Call center work can be tough, with challenging customers, strict schedules, and high stress. But it also offers opportunities for problem-solving, camaraderie, and the satisfaction of helping customers. If a call center glosses over these issues and sells itself as a fun, laid-back place to work, it will likely attract people unprepared for the realities of the job, leading to high turnover and low morale. On the other hand, if it presents a realistic picture of the work, emphasizing the opportunities for problem-solving and teamwork, it is more likely to attract individuals prepared for and even excited about the challenges, leading to a more motivated, satisfied workforce.

In an era of shiny perks and Instagram-worthy office spaces, painting a rosy picture is a temptation that is hard to resist. But the short-term gain in attracting applicants can lead to long-term pain in the form of high turnover, low morale, and an eroded culture. By making work about work again and embracing authenticity, we can build trust, attract the right talent, and foster an environment where employees are engaged, satisfied, and productive. In the end, businesses aren't just selling products or services; they're also selling the experience of work itself. Let's make sure we're selling the real thing.

8

YOU NEED JORDANS
AND PIPPENS

Kane's Analytical Standpoint

I know as much about basketball as I do about beetle-rearing. Despite my lack of anything resembling knowledge of the game of basketball, though, even I am familiar with the legendary duo of Michael Jordan and Scottie Pippen. Together, they propelled the Chicago Bulls to six NBA championships in the 1990s, both bringing a unique but complementary skill set to the game. Jordan, of course, was the unstoppable scorer and charismatic star, while Pippen, often in the shadows, was the versatile glue guy doing a little bit of everything to keep the team together. Applying this dynamic duo's concept to your business can yield spectacular results. Just as in basketball, where you need both high scorers and players who contribute in less flashy ways, your organization needs a blend of Jordans and Pippens.

Let's begin with the Jordans. These are the high-performing, high-impact individuals who can change the game single-handedly with their talents. They are the stars who drive revenues, spearhead innovation, and put your company on the map. Their charisma and dynamic abilities can often make them the face of the company.

However, like Jordan on the basketball court, these stars in your organization can't do everything on their own. They need the support of the Pippens—those individuals who may not be as flashy or as visible but are equally essential to the overall success of the business. The Pippens are the unsung heroes who do the so-called dirty work. They might be the ones coordinating logistics, maintaining quality control, handling customer service, or managing the day-to-day operations. While they may not frequently be in the spotlight, their work is the bedrock on which your company operates.

The Pippens understand that their role, although less glamorous, is vital for the smooth functioning of the organization. They are detail-oriented, process-driven individuals who keep the wheels turning while the Jordans are making the headlines. Their dedication, resilience, and commitment often form the backbone of the company. In truth, business leadership is about making sure your Pippens are appreciated and acknowledged. The Jordans of any organization are sure to get the plaudits. The Pippens, without effort on behalf of leadership, can feel neglected despite the high-value work they do.

Both Jordans and Pippens are crucial for a balanced and successful team. Just as a basketball team needs both the scoring ability of a star player and the utility of a role player, your organization needs the vision and ambition of the Jordans, coupled with the steady, relentless drive of the Pippens.

Building such a balanced team requires a deep understanding of your employees' unique abilities and how they fit into the larger organizational picture. As a leader, it's your job to identify your Jordans and your Pippens, to understand their respective strengths and how they can complement each other. Celebrate the big wins the Jordans bring, but also acknowledge the consistent contributions of the Pippens. Make sure your Pippens understand their value and feel appreciated. This balance in recognition fosters a positive work environment where everyone feels their role is essential to the company's success.

Remember it was the synergy between Jordan and Pippen that made the Chicago Bulls a dynasty in the 1990s. The same principle applies in business: by harmoniously blending the strengths of your Jordans and Pippens, your organization can reach unprecedented heights of success and make a lasting impact in your industry.

Building a successful team is not about amassing a group of superstars; it's about crafting a blend of talent where everyone knows their role and executes it to the best of their ability. It's about recognizing that while not everyone can be a Jordan, every Jordan needs a Pippen. And it is this unique blend of talent that creates truly great teams in sports, business, and beyond.

James's Street-Smart Opinion

We are two guys who don't know much about basketball, writing about basketball. I was lucky enough to grow up during the Jordan era, and while this is a personal opinion, it was the greatest era of basketball. I grew up in Detroit, and we had the Bad Boys. Also, let's not forget the early 2000s run—different game, different times, but lots of lessons indeed.

I founded a handful of recruiting companies before I could legally drink. Back in those days, I always had an eye for top talent. I would send my clients the top 5 percent in talent and say, "Hire this person, they are amazing!" Often, clients would say, "We can't afford them."

See, having eyes bigger than your stomach, as they say, doesn't work so well when you have a budget to maintain. As my companies grew and I became a little more business savvy, I realized you can't have a team of Jordans for a whole myriad of reasons.

First, you can't afford it. You'd have a cash flow problem instantly, burning cash in a burn barrel that won't even keep you warm. The second issue is, they won't get along. If you put five Jordans on a team, all they will do is argue, fight, and spend more time posturing up than posting up. There is where you find a balance, a delicate blend in which the sauce doesn't end up too salty but is also flavorful enough not to taste bland. It's not exactly the easiest balance to maintain, but it's possible.

We talk about the 20 percent rule a lot: have 20 percent killers on your team and 80 percent role players. Spend a lot on the killers and hire budget-friendly role players to fill the remaining 80 percent of your workforce. Using simple math, it's a pack of five people with one killer and four support staff. The killer gets to lead as they want to and one of the four support staff will likely be the one to get their hands dirty as they want to become a killer one day. That's the thing with the killers. They are so busy talking about their Harvard MBA that they don't want to get dirt under their fingernails. Well, they'll likely just get a manicure, but you know what I mean. The bigger the ego, the less likely they will be to do the scut work, so you need people who are willing to show up and show out.

This is pretty much how the business world has operated for a hundred years. The game hasn't changed, but the narrative makes it seem like it has. The biggest issue you face today is that the 80 percent often think they are killers and want to be treated accordingly. It's a strange hierarchy, but it works. All killers won't work. All role players won't work. You need a leader, a go-getter, and some followers, and most things fall into place. But keep in mind that your killer can't be selfish. Even Jordan passed the ball at the right time.

9

YOU'RE ONLY AS STRONG AS YOUR WEAKEST LINK

James's Bold Insight

If you look at the classic boy bands, you'll see there was always a weak link. You had the star singer who was also the heartthrob. Then you had two or three dudes with their own skills. Finally, you had one performer that no one understood why he was there. Yet the band survived and went on to make millions of dollars. This lasted for a while, until the lead singer decided to go solo, leaving everyone else to basically start an OnlyFans account, or worse, a podcast.

Most departments are built in a similar way in today's world—ideally, one Jordan for every four Pippens. The problem happens when one of those Pippens isn't carrying his weight. This is often someone with poor tenure, who was maybe a "cheaper hire" or was hired too quickly.

This issue can also happen when a company is growing fast and outgrows its people at the same time. This is an important lesson you'll hear us talk about often. As you grow, help people grow and take them with you for the ride. Otherwise you have to leave them behind, or worse, they slow you down and your company will never fully reach its potential. We tend to see smaller companies dealing with this more frequently. If you're a Fortune 500 company with 10,000 employees, one person not carrying their weight won't even be noticed. But if an employee behaves that way at a ten-, twenty-, or even fifty-person company, everyone feels it.

Another way to address this is to look for bottlenecks. When we are offering growth consulting at Daggerfinn, one of the first things we do is look for bottlenecks. We identify the barriers to growth, then figure out a plan of attack to address that bottleneck so we can scale.

For example, what if your sales pipeline is a bottleneck? Instead of one sales rep, do you have two sales reps at $75,000 to handle sales, or do you need someone more experienced and strategic who costs $150,000? Do you need three phone pounders at $50,000 each who are basically telemarketers? This last option works well if the product or service sells itself. This all depends on the bottleneck. Is the bottleneck the lack of man hours to generate more sales leads, or do you have a solid sales funnel but the person in the role cannot close the sale?

Business consultants often talk about hitting the wall at $5 million, $10 million, and $25 million. Or they mention hitting the wall at twenty-five employees, fifty employees, or one hundred employees. Companies frequently get stuck here for years, bouncing up and down 10–15 percent, but they can't consistently grow without taking a step back.

Most of this is attributed to failure to address the weak links. Sometimes, you don't know you have them or you don't know how to identify them. At other times, it may mean taking action that would affect a loyal employee's career, so you avoid it for as long as you can. If you don't address the bottlenecks, you'll continue to struggle. Ignoring problems doesn't make them go away—in fact, they usually get worse.

Kane's Methodical Perspective

If you've ever watched Lionel Messi play soccer, you'll have noticed that his talent is beyond extraordinary. Yet, despite Messi's prowess, his teams—be it his club team or his national team—cannot rely on him alone to win. Why is that? Simply put, a soccer team is only as good as its weakest link.

You see, in soccer and in business, no matter how talented your star player or how efficient your leading department, the performance of the weakest link determines the pace of the game or the growth of the company. This principle, referred to as the theory of constraints in operations management, holds that the pace of a process is dictated not by the fastest activity, but by the slowest.

Take a factory assembly line as an example. If one machine can process one hundred units per hour, but the subsequent one can handle only fifty, the overall output isn't one hundred units per hour—it's fifty. The faster machine can churn out units all it wants, but unless the slower machine speeds up, there's going to be a pileup. This is known as a bottleneck, and it can exist anywhere in an organization—from manufacturing to customer service, from marketing to delivery. The key to improving overall productivity lies in identifying these bottlenecks and eliminating them.

Think of your business as a chain, with each department or individual representing a link. This chain can bear only as much weight as the weakest link can handle before it snaps. By strengthening the weakest link, the overall chain becomes stronger. That's why, in management, there's an absolute necessity to continuously identify and bolster the weakest links, in order to lift the overall business performance.

Drawing parallels to our soccer team analogy, consider how Messi's teams adapt their strategy. Yes, they leverage Messi's phenomenal skills to the maximum. However, they also work on shoring up the defense, improving the midfield play, and sharpening the skills of other forwards. If they didn't, Messi's brilliance would amount to naught if the team conceded goals or if no other player could score.

Let's look at a real-world business example: Ford Motor Company. Henry Ford realized traditional car assembly methods created bottlenecks that slowed production and raised costs. His solution? The assembly line. By breaking the car-building process down into smaller tasks and assigning each task to a different worker, Ford dramatically increased production speed and decreased costs. In your business, strengthening the weakest link starts by identifying the current bottlenecks. Once you've identified these, you can address them—be it through process improvement, employee training, technology upgrades, or hiring new talent.

It's worth remembering that, just like in soccer, every player in a business has a role to play. Each department, no matter how seemingly small or insignificant, contributes to the overall performance of the organization. It's time to scan your business for bottlenecks and underperformers. Encourage your team to identify areas where they are stuck and need assistance. Let the brilliance of your top performers inspire, not intimidate, the rest of the team.

10

HIRING, HAVE IT YOUR WAY

Kane's Strategic Viewpoint

Hiring is one of the most challenging tasks a business faces, and it's only getting trickier as the labor market evolves. Today's working landscape looks vastly different from that of the past, with an increasing shift from large, sprawling workforces to nimble, high-performing teams. The future of work points to organizations resembling elite SWAT teams, composed of a compact group of diversified, skilled employees. Why this move? Because finding the right fit—both in skills and in culture—is hard. Moreover, in a world where job tenure is consistently declining, companies can no longer bank on employees sticking around for an entire career.

Traditionally, businesses followed a model of scaling up—the larger the workforce, the better the results. Executives were compensated based on the size of their teams. Bigger was synonymous with better, reflecting success and growth. However, modern workplaces are beginning to question this assumption.

This shift can be attributed to several factors, one being the challenge of hiring, itself. It's no secret that finding the right fit is hard. In an age of abundant choices, candidates are looking beyond salary and job descriptions. They seek roles that align with their values, offer growth opportunities, and promise a good work-life balance. This search for fit goes both ways. Companies strive to find candidates who align with their culture, vision, and long-term goals.

Hiring isn't merely about filling a position. It's about finding the right person who can contribute meaningfully to the company's mission. In this context, size doesn't always equal strength. A smaller team of dedicated, skilled professionals can often deliver better results than a large, disjointed workforce.

The decline in job tenure is playing a significant role in this shift too. Employees sticking around for an entire career is increasingly rare. A study by the Bureau of Labor Statistics found that younger baby boomers held an average of 12.3 jobs from ages eighteen to fifty-two. And this number is likely to increase for younger generations, with job-hopping becoming more prevalent. This frequent job transition is forcing businesses to rethink their hiring strategies. In a rapidly changing marketplace, hiring for longevity might not always be the smartest move. Instead, hiring individuals with the right skills and cultural fit becomes paramount.

Let's consider the elite SWAT team analogy. A SWAT team isn't large; instead, it comprises a select group of highly trained individuals, each with a specific set of skills. They are incredibly effective because of their training, synergy, and ability to quickly adapt to changing situations. Each member is there because they are the best at what they do, and they fit seamlessly into the team's overall mission.

Businesses can learn a lot from this model. Hiring a small, diverse team of individuals who are experts in their respective fields can lead to higher efficiency and productivity. Each team member brings something unique to the table, fostering a culture of learning and mutual respect. Plus, smaller teams allow for more agile decision-making and quicker adaptability in a constantly evolving business landscape.

That's not to say businesses shouldn't scale or grow their workforces when necessary. The key lies in smart hiring—building a solid core team of diverse individuals who share the company's values and vision. These core members can then become culture carriers, setting the tone for future hires and ensuring the preservation of the company's culture as it grows.

As the world changes, so too does the art of hiring. Businesses must navigate the delicate balance of finding individuals with the right skills, who also align with the company culture, all while bearing in mind the shorter job tenures of the modern world. It's a challenging task, but remember a smaller, committed, and skilled workforce can often pack a bigger punch than a large, disjointed one. Much like an elite SWAT team, an organization's strength lies in its people—their skills, their dedication, and their ability to work together toward a shared goal.

James's Unfiltered Take

I'm thinking back to a conversation I overheard at a bar in Chicago. We were out at a group happy hour, probably at RPM Steak or Bavatte's, around 4:00 or 5:00 p.m. on a weekday, a common time to see people going on quick dates for a cocktail or meeting their friends for some appetizers on the cheap.

I remember the line because it was so true and it also made me laugh. These two people were talking rather loudly about their exes; their cocktails must have kicked in. This is only an assumption, but it sounded like one or both of them may have been divorced. Over the loud crowd at the bar and the music in the background, it sounded like he asked her where it all went wrong. She responded with something along the lines of "I married him for his hair and he was funny." She had come to find out that didn't equate to marrying a great partner.

I had to ad-lib there a little bit, but we've all heard similar lines from our friends and family over the years as they got divorced. As humans, we often make decisions based on things that shouldn't be in the equation. In this case, sure, you probably need to be attracted to the person, and they should share most or at least some of your values, but there's that old cliché that "beauty is only skin deep."

I use a lot of relationship analogies because I've always seen so many similarities when it comes to hiring. When hiring, it's easy to look at things on a surface level and not dig deeper. You should try to figure out if this person has the things that matter in order to succeed.

The things I discuss in my forthcoming book *Headwind*, which is about navigating life in your twenties and thirties, all align with this. I write about evaluating a future partner. People in their twenties are typically not who they will be in their forties and fifties, but it seems like no one's looking down the road more than a couple of days at a time anymore. Sure, you may be attracted to them and they're funny, but do they have everything else you need to sustain a long, loving relationship?

Is this person kind and empathetic? Are they thoughtful and mindful? What is their relationship with their parents, and did their parents influence them in a good or bad way? Will this person be a good parent? When times get tough, how will this person react? Do they have a passion or dream they are chasing?

There are many things you should look at before you say, "I do." But rarely do people do that. They say things like "this person makes me happy" and "I enjoy being with them." Or, you have that friend who simply says, "because they're hot af." Sometimes that works, but it doesn't seem to work that often.

Let's apply this concept to hiring. One thing we know after being involved in the executive search business for a long time is that tenure is extremely important. Now on social media and, to be blunt, media in general, there is a push to say it's okay to job-hop. That's what candidates want to hear, and the news media sites push that narrative because, in search of ratings, they push things people want to hear. Come to find out no one really cares about the truth anymore; they only care about views and clicks.

The number one reason for rejection of candidates is lack of tenure. As an employer, why would you hire someone who doesn't have a history of sticking around more than one or two years? You spent all that time and money to interview and hire someone, just to see them flee nine to twelve months later?

Come on, now. You can't sustain or grow a business when you're turning over your entire team every twenty-four months. Hiring managers have gotten a lot smarter. In the past, hiring managers thought they could change this person or offer them a better environment so they would stay.

But now there's been so much research done on behavior and behavioral economics that we know the truth. It comes down to this: an established pattern of constant job-hopping will not end with you.

Why do hiring managers care so much about tenure? Often, job-hopping is a sign that this person has some kind of behavioral issue. If you have ever managed a team, you know what I'm talking about. These are the people who drill holes in the boat. They bring everyone around them down and have a negative influence on the team and your company. They can't get their work done on time or, if they do, it's sloppy. They don't show up to work on time, or they've done something else that has gotten them written up by HR multiple times.

Kane ran a survey a little while ago, and the results were very interesting. When polled, 80%+ of managers \ coworkers said poor behavior, not lack of intelligence, is why people fail at their jobs. Now that's not the only reason. We could write a whole book on the ins and outs of why people don't succeed. After several decades of talking to people in HR and receiving their feedback, you surely understand the trends, though.

When hiring, you can't set a low bar for key positions. There are times when you just need to fill a seat and you're better off having a warm body in that seat than nobody. Anyone in the business world understands that well, especially when demand is through the roof. But for those key players, that bar needs to be high, and you shouldn't make exceptions.

Also, when you're interviewing, do you really understand why you're asking these questions? Have you ever gone through the interview with the hiring team to figure out what questions you're going to ask and what answers you're looking for?

We have learned over the years that people jump online, grab a set of interview questions, and ask them. Then they make a hire based on whether or not they like the person. They didn't make the hire based on the questions and how the candidate answered them. This is beginning to sound like marrying someone for their hair and good jokes.

You also can't fall into the trap of thinking someone's going to succeed in your company because they worked for a big name. Hiring managers will find someone who worked at XYZ Fortune 500 thinking that if they can survive there, they can survive in a smaller company. That's not true. It's often harder to survive in a smaller company because employees don't have the luxury of concentrating on only one or two tasks, whereas Fortune 500 companies sometimes have people focused on just one thing.

In the executive search business, we often see this with supply chain executives. At a large company, depending on how they silo, the SVP of the supply chain may have a handful of executives under them. They may have a procurement officer, a logistics executive, a materials executive, a warehouse executive, and, if it's a manufacturing company, a director or VP of production or a high-level ERP person dealing with something like SAP.

At the smaller company, the supply chain executive may fulfill all of these functions with a handful of less-qualified managers below them. If you're that procurement officer at a Fortune 500 company and you're walking into a manufacturing company where you need to oversee materials, warehousing, logistics, and transportation plus ERP, let's just say we hope you're up for the chaos, because most are not.

Along with big corporate names, big college or university names should also not be weighted too heavily during the interview process.

Education used to mean something. If you saw someone with a four-year degree from a good college, you expected they could do things such as write a coherent paragraph or use critical thinking to solve a problem. That's no longer the case. It seems even some of the best colleges have turned into degree mills. How can you hire someone as a project manager who can't write a detailed and articulate report? We used to get excited when we saw those big college names on résumés. Now they don't mean much. The only thing we can rely on, to a point, is candidates' accomplishments in the real world.

Don't get sold on charisma either. We've all had that interviewee come in with the big, bright smile, and they look like such a pleasure to work with that you want to hire them on the spot. All of a sudden, you lower your standards on tenure. You're no longer focused on the metrics and KPIs they achieved in prior positions. You stop asking follow-up questions to the answers they gave you because you're enamored with them. Once again, you will often end up disappointed with these hires. Stick to your hiring process like your eggs stick to your stainless steel pans (FYI, just use more butter next time).

We could write a book just on how to hire. We have touched in this book on some of the things we commonly see. These are also some of the processes and pitfalls we've used to make great hires and make our turnover rate one of the lowest in our industry. It took over a decade to develop this process, not to mention the fact that we have to constantly train people to use it. If you deviate from it, even a little, it fails.

As I mentioned, in the same way you would vet somebody to be a future partner and / or parent, you would evaluate a new hire. You are evaluating both quantitative and qualitative aspects of this person. If we could all see two to five years down the road, none of us would make a mistake. No matter how much due diligence you do, you're going to make a bad hire every once in a while. But if you keep the bar high and stick to your process, don't let yourself get emotional, and stop relying on your gut, you will start making better hires. We always like to say never to settle, but in this job market, that may be tough. When it comes to that inner circle, though, don't waver. You have to keep grinding away until you find that ideal match.

11

ONCE YOU HAVE THEM, KEEP THEM

James's Assertive Thoughts

It's infuriating. You likely spend two or three months doing interviews, negotiating a job offer, then waiting for the successful candidate to put in their two-week notice at their prior employer. Finally, they come to work for you. You spend another three to six months getting them up to speed. Just before they spread their wings, they fly their ass right over to another company.

You are back at ground zero. This is why turnover is so damn expensive. And how do you grow your department or company if every nine months you're hitting a reset switch? You never get momentum or the opportunity to make the changes you need to drive the company forward.

For all the years we spent in the recruiting business, I can probably think of a hundred conversations I got into with HR and the C-Suite about retention. Headhunting isn't cheap, and when you're doing retained executive searches, it costs one hell of a chunk of money. We would tell customers, in an ideal world, they would hang on to people so they didn't have to pay us all that money. That's why I engaged in those conversations. I realized most of these companies have not put a tremendous amount of thought into retention.

We like to think of retention as boxing. If you're constantly on the ropes or in the corners, it's only a matter of time before you get your ass knocked out. You can't spend all your time doing defense. That allows you to limit the damage, but does not give you a chance to win. You have to get in there and throw some punches. Offense is defense in this case. When it comes to retention, most companies spend their time on the ropes or in the corners taking liver shots and getting their chin checked. As you can imagine, this doesn't work out for them in the end.

Let's talk about tools that help with retention. When we're working on an employer branding project, typically that includes surveys we developed with IO psychologists. We even use an AI component developed in-house to double-check sentiment. We learned over the years that almost every company uses surveys, then twelve months later, nothing has improved. If you're not really listening to people about how they feel about your culture and your company, you're never going to make the necessary changes to keep them. You're just collecting data, which you poorly interpret. It's not working, is it? You can use these tools, but you need to take action based on the insights you gather. We constantly talk about the inner circle. Who's paying attention and actively trying to keep those people on board?

It's not always about money, but in this inflationary world, money certainly matters. How does your employees' compensation stack up against that offered by the local or regional employer of choice? How does your team feel about the current vacation policy or their ability to spend some of their time working for a cause they care about?

For everyone you're trying to keep, do you have some kind of plan that shows them where they can grow? Now, not every position has a growth plan; sometimes, a position is just that. At other times, there are clear paths upward, but have you communicated them clearly? People tend to leave when they feel undervalued or like they have run out of runway.

When you have someone amazing on your team and they're running out of runway, build a longer runway. This may mean creating a new position or expanding part of your business in order to accommodate this person who could help you grow top-line revenue.

In a strange way, in the post-COVID world, people have lost ambition and motivation. They're more worried about work-life balance and life experiences. Fewer care about the corner office and joining the C-Suite. But that doesn't mean everybody feels that way. Many people on your team are still trying to get somewhere. And if they feel as if they're never going to get anywhere in their current role, you're going to lose them.

Never be afraid to lose the people you don't want anyway. That's a giant money suck or, as we say, it's like burning cash in a barrel. Some positions will always see high turnover, and you have to learn to do business in that environment. When you lose a bottom or middle player, look at it as an opportunity to upgrade. If you're paying $75,000 for someone who was a low or middle player at best, maybe now is a good time to look at someone at $82,500 who can really make a difference.

Always have a list of that inner circle, of the people you never want to lose. Always understand their expectations and where they want to go.

Always take the pulse of that group. If they feel like they're part of something, they are well compensated, and they have a clear path to achieve their goals, they'll likely stick around for decades.

Don't just send surveys out, make broad assumptions, and convince yourself your company is such an amazing place to work that no one would want to leave. If that were true in any way, shape, or form, most companies wouldn't have a turnover issue in the first place.

Kane's Systematic Analysis

The word *retention* is often thrown around in the business world, but its implications run far deeper than most hiring managers realize. It's not simply about keeping employees on your payroll; it's about actively ensuring their happiness, engagement, and growth within your company. The retention of top talent should be at the forefront of every manager's strategic plan, because even if you've successfully attracted the best minds, keeping them is an entirely different game.

Rookie managers often make a common mistake: they assume that once they have a fantastic team in place, their work stops there. They believe great employees will stay indefinitely, content with the status quo. However, this couldn't be further from the truth. Keeping your best employees is not a passive process—it requires consistent, active efforts from leaders. Great talents need more than a paycheck to stay engaged and loyal; they need a compelling reason to commit their careers to your organization.

Many times, we've asked our clients if they have any intuition as to why their best employees go to their competitors, and the response is that they were offered a few bucks an hour more. This is, more often than not, blatantly incorrect and misinformed. Remember people will only tell you—especially during an exit interview—what they think you want to hear so they can get out of there as quickly and painlessly as possible.

The modern work environment is rapidly evolving. Employees, especially top performers, know their worth and seek roles that provide not just remuneration, but opportunities for growth, a sense of purpose, and a strong work-life balance. A static environment or lack of development opportunities can easily push top talents to seek greener pastures. As a leader, you have a responsibility to foster a dynamic environment that actively promotes these values.

First, invest in professional development. Help your employees grow by providing them with ample learning opportunities and resources. This can be in the form of training programs, workshops, or even an environment that encourages self-teaching. Remember when your employees grow, so does your organization.

Second, cultivate a sense of purpose. Top talents often seek work that aligns with their personal values and passions. Make it a point to articulate your organization's mission and values clearly and demonstrate how each role contributes to the greater good. By doing so, you'll help employees see the impact of their work and provide them with a compelling reason to stay.

It's also crucial to create a culture of recognition. Everyone wants to feel valued and appreciated for their work. Regularly acknowledging your team's efforts, big or small, will help them feel seen and appreciated.

This can take the form of public recognition in team meetings, a personal thank-you note, or even formal rewards and bonuses.

Last, foster open communication. Employees who feel their voices are heard are more likely to stay loyal. Regularly seek out your team's feedback and opinions on workplace matters. This not only improves your business operations, but also empowers employees, helping them feel invested in the company's future.

Retention is indeed an active pursuit, requiring attention and dedication from management. But the efforts are worthwhile. The benefits of retaining top talent are manifold, from preserving organizational knowledge and promoting stability to saving costs associated with hiring and training new employees.

Never take your top performers for granted. They are your organization's most valuable assets. In a world where talented individuals have countless opportunities, companies that make the active effort to engage and retain their employees will come out on top. A satisfied, loyal employee is an invaluable resource—take the steps to ensure they stay that way.

12

OFFBOARDING: COACHING UP OR OUT

Kane's Careful Approach

When we talk about employees and workplace culture, much attention is given to the entrance—onboarding, to be precise. But equally important, if less emphasized, is the exit, or offboarding. Offboarding is as much a part of the employee life cycle as onboarding, and the way a company handles this stage can have far-reaching implications.

It is crucial for us as leaders to approach offboarding with the same level of care and commitment as we do recruitment and retention. Employees might be leaving your organization, but their experiences and opinions will continue to impact your company's reputation and its ability to attract future talent.

When an employee decides to move on, conducting an exit interview is a common practice. This can provide valuable insights about the workplace environment, job satisfaction, and reasons for leaving. However, it's important to remember that not all feedback you receive during these exit interviews is going to be entirely accurate or reliable.

Why? People are inherently diplomatic, and departing employees in particular may tell you what they think you want to hear. They may be concerned about burning bridges or impacting references, so they might refrain from providing honest criticism. It's important to keep this in mind when interpreting the feedback from exit interviews. Treat the information as a piece of the puzzle, but don't consider it the complete picture.

Offboarding also ensures the smooth transition of the exiting employee's responsibilities to other team members. This might mean documenting workflows and handing over client relationships, essentially ensuring the least possible disruption to business operations. This is a two-way street where the outgoing employee needs to cooperate, but it also necessitates proactive planning from the management side.

Furthermore, offboarding is an opportunity for closure for both the employer and the employee. It's a time to appreciate the contributions the departing employee has made and wish them well in their future endeavors. This leaves a positive lasting impression and maintains good relations between the company and its former employees. Remember your company's alumni can become valuable assets, potentially referring new clients, endorsing your workplace, or even returning as "boomerang employees" in the future.

On the other hand, there are times when offboarding isn't the result of an employee's decision to leave, but rather a strategic move on the company's part. This is commonly known as "coaching out." In these instances, the company identifies underperforming employees and, instead of immediate termination, provides them an opportunity to improve. Clear expectations are set, and if the employee cannot meet these standards, they're guided toward an exit.

Coaching out can be a sensitive process, and it's important to approach it with respect and fairness. It's not about shaming or cornering an employee; it's about recognizing that the individual might be a better fit elsewhere. The intention should always be to set every team member up for success, whether within your organization or beyond it.

In essence, offboarding, whether through exit or coaching out, should be conducted with grace, professionalism, and mutual respect. Remember, the manner in which an employee exits your organization is as much a reflection of your company's culture as the way they were onboarded and managed. It's a process that demands thoughtful attention, and, when done right, it can reinforce your company's reputation as a fair, respectful, and desirable place to work.

James's Gritty Observation

We talked about how much time you're going to spend on employer branding and hiring, but how much thought have you put into the offboarding process?

Well, you'll never avoid bad online reviews. If you make missteps during offboarding, you're almost certain to get one. More important, beyond bad online reviews that affect your employer brand, you have to keep in mind that the people you let go will likely still talk to the people you retain. As stated earlier in this book, when you let negative people go, two or three other people within their clique will also leave in the coming months. The same thing happens if the turnover is voluntary.

The problem comes when you part ways with somebody and they're in contact with more than just your little group. People tend to embellish what really happened and, as an employer, you end up stuck in the middle because you typically have to keep things private, especially if something's in their employee file. Employers get put in this position because people can leave and say whatever they want, make up lies, and even slander you. You don't have much of a defense. Sure, you can fight back, and sometimes you have to make an example out of somebody and go to court. You can't be afraid to do that; just pick the right time.

This all goes better if you mitigate this situation from the beginning. You can do a couple of things. Which you choose depends on if you're dealing with a performance issue or a behavior one. Now it's possible you're dealing with both at the same time, but when addressing a performance issue, you can likely start by putting someone on a performance improvement plan (PIP). Set a ninety-day goal to get this person back on track with very well-defined milestones. This usually lights the fire under somebody's butt and gets them moving. On the other hand, some people believe this is the first step to firing them, so they'll start looking for a job and possibly leave on their own. In an ideal world, this is somebody you want to keep on the team; you just need them to perform at an adequate level. But if they show you they straight up don't care, that gives you a reason to coach them out.

Again, with the bulk of employee failures in the workplace being based on behavior, this is another uphill battle to which you have to adapt. We actually created a whole new startup based on coaching employees, especially from the younger generations. This concept centers around teaching people how to succeed in the modern-day workforce. Dealing with behavior issues that make people nearly unemployable only leads you down one path.

Another thing you can do, if it's performance related, is to figure out if this employee is in the right seat. Sometimes you have somebody who is really down for your culture, who works hard, and who really wants to be there. Unfortunately, they just can't thrive in that particular role. The answer isn't always to let somebody go. If this employee is good for your culture, look around and see what other roles you can move them into in order to give them another shot.

But, when it comes down to it, if this employee is extremely negative and causing a toxic work environment, you have to get a plan together so you can part ways. What's the best way to mitigate issues when parting ways? One is using an outplacement service. One of our companies offers outplacement services, and we have come to find out that many companies don't even use this. Many managers have never even heard of it. Now this isn't a pitch to use us; it's just advice to consider this type of service, and I'm going to tell you why.

Let me use another dating and relationship reference here; some say the fastest way to get over someone is to find someone else. Do you remember your days as a teenager when your heart was broken and you spent all day and night thinking about this person you couldn't have anymore? Maybe you were the one who broke somebody's heart and they had those same feelings, which eventually turned to hate. How many times have you heard someone say how much they hate their ex?

See, outplacement services are designed to coach someone through the transition of losing their job, getting back on their feet, and finding a new job fast. This may include helping them write a proper résumé, figuring out which companies to apply for, interview coaching, and even how to negotiate a good offer. The goal here is to keep them motivated and to get them a new job ASAP so they're not sitting around thinking about how much they hate your company. Don't give them time to stew, firing off texts to all of your employees and trying to get them to quit. Another benefit of outplacement services is, if you get them back to work faster, that could lower your unemployment insurance rate, but you need to check with your CPA on that one.

There is also the reputation management side to this. Many companies offer outplacement services as part of a severance package. Typically, to take part of that severance package, the employee signs a release form that says they're not going to sue you in the future. You may even be able to include a clause about them not making disparaging remarks about your company. Check with your lawyer on this one. These things are worth looking into as you offer an outplacement and severance package. At the end of the day, this is all about protecting your company and your brand.

You should consider a few other things as well. As we know, companies love running surveys about everything under the sun, but they're terrible at connecting the dots. An exit interview can provide great insights. Now this typically works with someone who is choosing to leave on their own, and not so much with someone you've had to let go for other reasons.

An exit interview will often be given by someone's manager or HR. When it is done in person, you'll find that, many times, the individual is trying to avoid confrontation and they're just telling you things you want to hear. There is no guarantee of more honest answers from an exit survey, but since, unlike in an exit interview, they're not sitting across from another human being, it's possible to get slightly more insightful data. Then the question is, what are you going to do with those data? Well, that's a whole other problem.

Last, we can talk a little bit about the coaching-out process. While a PIP may be the beginning of coaching out someone who is struggling with behavioral issues, there are other times when you just don't have room for somebody. They didn't do anything wrong, or maybe they're not the best fit skill-wise for the position you have them in, but you have nowhere else for them to go.

Some companies in this situation give the employee ninety days to find another job. The manager has a conversation with the employee about how they're not an ideal fit for the organization, but they want to make the transition as smooth as possible. An agreement that the employee will continue to do their job and not drag other people down gives the employee time to seek work with another company that fits them better. Again, run these concepts by your attorney as employment laws vary from state to state, but this is a nice way to show you're fair and balanced and you do care about people.

Another method of coaching out is to mentor people. Someone may often tell you they have always wanted to do sales, but, after observing them for six months, you realize sales really isn't the right field for them. Another part of coaching out is just being honest with somebody and giving them direction. You're going to see this happen more often with somebody in the first three to five years of their career, maybe even up to the first ten. You don't want to rain on anyone's parade or crush someone's dream, but if someone continues to struggle in a role, they don't lack intelligence, and it's not a behavioral issue, then someone has to tell them that maybe that isn't where they will succeed. No one likes to be told they can't do something, but I'm sure all of us at some point in our lives wish we had gotten that kind of advice.

The lesson here is, if you have negativity in your company, you have to find ways to remove it and to mitigate any legal or employer branding issues if you can. If you have good people, try to coach them up if they're struggling to perform. If you have the right person in the wrong role, find another role for them within your company. And if you no longer have a role for someone who is not causing harm, find a way to help them transition. You want to be a good company and a good person to people who are good to you. This protects your employer brand, keeps your turnover low, and creates an environment where people want to work.

13

MANAGING PRODUCTIVITY IN AN UNPRODUCTIVE WORLD

James's Direct Interpretation

Take one look at the chart below and you can see how ugly this conversation is going to get. It shows you historical data on wages versus productivity.

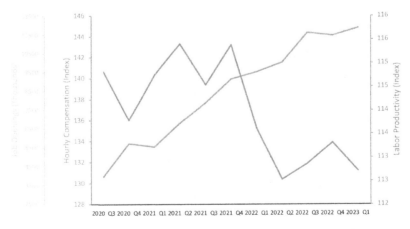

Source: Daggerfinn Analysis of Bureau of Labor Statistics Data

We got the sense, going back to about 2015, that worker productivity was dropping even if we didn't see it on our own internal charts. When we talked to people who ran departments or had P&L responsibility, the gist of those conversations was that output was beginning to suffer.

If you've ever been in a retail environment or restaurant and suffered from poor service, you probably weren't surprised to see workers standing around and playing on their cell phones. Technology has made us more productive in many ways and at the same time has made us more distracted than ever. We can't even focus on our work we're getting paid to do. For example, just recently, I was at a juice joint to get a shake. I waited for five minutes while the guy in the back room played TikTok videos on his phone. Finally, as he saw me waving, he ran up and apologized. Come on, man, really?

But it's not just technology. In our country, we went from a culture that was about hard work and achieving high goals to a culture that is more about doing as little as possible while just trying to get by. Then COVID came and amplified this whole scenario. When you look at that chart and you see productivity going down and wages going up, it should give you a sinking feeling in your stomach. If you're any kind of seasoned business operator, you know this is not sustainable in the long run. And if it does become sustainable, it's because you've begun to replace unproductive workers with AI and robots.

The Western world has a culture problem with a direct effect on productivity and output. Between parents and colleges, the next generation is not entering the workforce with the attitude they need to succeed. New grads are stepping in with no experience and demanding to be managers within twelve months. To top it off, many of them don't understand how important punctuality and professionalism are or what it takes to lead a team. How do they plan to lead people if they can't even manage themselves?

From productivity issues to building the next generation of managers, you as a hiring manager in this new economy certainly have your work cut out for you. One of the keys to building a productive workforce is not to have any junk time. Some people call it junk time; others call it bench time. Let's just say if you're paying someone for forty hours of work, you need to get forty hours' worth of work out of them.

Make sure to communicate this up front before you even make an offer to someone. What you say and what people think they hear are usually two different things. Our example from earlier of a vacation policy applies here. If you mention you don't have a formal vacation policy and how much vacation employees get is based on merit, this could be interpreted differently depending on who is listening. While you were clear about the vacation policy, many people hear they have unlimited vacation time and think they will come in, have no tenure with your company, and take eight weeks off. We talk about this often because we have heard this story so many times from clients.

This is why we say when you're hiring, be very upfront about culture and expectations. For one of our companies, we've even gotten to the point where as part of the offer letter, we spell out exactly what the job is. If you don't, you'll quickly find out how wild people's minds can run and what they come up with, which usually doesn't align with what you told them.

Companies are also fighting the work-from-home culture. Business owners find it funny when they read online that managers just want employees in the office so they can control them. When you read this, you realize most of these people have no idea what kinds of conversations are going on in the boardroom. They think they know what it is to be an executive or in the C-Suite or a business owner, but they really have no idea. At the end of the day, business owners don't want the expense of the office space. If I could save $500,000 a year by not having an office space and everyone got their work done well and on-time from home while keeping our culture, why the hell would I keep spending $500,000 a year on an office? If I do, it's because I see value in it.

When we talk to HR executives and business owners, what it comes down to is productivity of today isn't matching that of the pre-COVID world. And as much as people say they get more work done from home, all you have to do is keep looking at the productivity chart to figure out the answer. Many times, when we're talking to executives or department managers at large companies, they tell us they now need twelve people to do the same work that ten used to do. Again, the math doesn't lie. If everyone was just as productive from home, they wouldn't need two extra people to do the same amount of work. Wait. If people are more productive working from home, you only need eight people instead of ten. See what I did there?

Losing culture is another issue caused by not having an office. It's tough to build culture over a Zoom call, or to get to know anybody at all, really. Let me use another relationship reference: it's like a long-distance relationship where you only see your partner twice a year, and we know those never work out.

The cost of working from home isn't just productivity, though. Companies are now learning that, without being in the office, it's difficult to bring up the next generation of managers. You have to be together in person to learn how people lead and to see how they deal with their teams. How do you develop emotional intelligence if you're never together in person to really get to know somebody? We think back to how much knowledge was transferred to our team as we built up our managers, who now have become directors and vice presidents. Those working from home just don't get the same benefit of that transfer of knowledge and witnessing leadership. We don't want to make the chapter about this, but as we talk about productivity, all of this kind of ties together and you should be aware of it.

Looking forward, you're not going to be able to pay people forty-hour salaries and get only fifteen to eighteen hours of work out of them. We've even heard some managers say if employees want to work eighteen hours, we're only going to pay them for eighteen hours.

Maybe it's time we move away from the forty-hour salary and pay for time spent working. That's where modern-day culture is going. If people want to work as little as possible in order to have more free time, maybe we need to tear down the forty-hour salary and move to hourly pay. We don't think everybody wants that, but since COVID, that has definitely been the sentiment among a large part of the workforce.

So you're faced with figuring out how to deal with low productivity, which means you're going to have shrinking margins or you have to continue to raise prices. The next option is to hold your workforce accountable. "I'm paying you for forty hours of work; we need forty hours worth of productive work." Don't give people junk or bench time. This isn't a large tech company; we cannot afford nap time around here.

This may require you to combine two roles into one if possible. But you can't have people sitting idle for 50 percent of the week while they're eating up your payroll money. This is why assembly lines worked so well back in the day. Whether or not people wanted to work, in forty-five seconds, another car was coming down the line. They had to do their job. It didn't allow for any idle time, but, in a way, that also allowed the company to pay a better salary due to the improved productivity.

Which brings us back to that chart. We all know what happens if wages continue to go up and productivity continues to go down. So the best thing you can do is work diligently to create a culture in your company that was built around hard work. Clearly college didn't show the newest generation in the workforce the way or teach them the behaviors they need to succeed in a company like yours. It's unfortunate that no one ever taught them those things, but someone's going to have to. And, as leaders, we say there's no time like the present.

Kane's Measured Opinion

Productivity, the heartbeat of any thriving economy, has been on a some-what declining trajectory over the past half decade or so. This decline in productivity is not just a statistical aberration or a temporary glitch—it is a trend, a changing dynamic in the workforce that has been amplified and accelerated by the seismic shift in working patterns instigated by the COVID-19 pandemic.

The way people view work and what they seek from an employer-employee relationship has undergone a tangible shift. In the flurry of change, the value of sheer hard work has seemingly diminished. Instead, a growing chorus is advocating for coasting along and prioritizing other aspects of life over career advancement. This new attitude is undoubtedly influenced by the events of the past few years, which have prompted many to reassess their priorities and personal goals.

While this perspective is not without merit—after all, life is indeed about more than just work—it does raise questions about the long-term implications for individual careers and overall economic productivity. The adage "you reap what you sow" comes to mind, and it might hold the key to understanding the future implications of this productivity paradigm shift.

To be clear, coasting along is not synonymous with laziness. Rather, it reflects a choice to allocate one's time and energy differently than traditional norms. But what happens when this coasting period extends from months into years, particularly early on in one's career? The concern lies not with the fact that people are reevaluating their work-life equation, but with the potential consequences of these decisions.

Professional growth, like many aspects of life, thrives on momentum. The foundational knowledge and skills gained in the early years of one's career often lay the groundwork for future advancement. Choosing to coast during these formative years brings a risk of stunting professional growth and limiting future opportunities. Furthermore, from a broader perspective, a decline in workforce productivity could impact economic growth, business competitiveness, and ultimately the standard of living.

As we navigate these changing work dynamics, it is worth remembering that while productivity may have a new look in today's evolving workforce, its importance remains undiminished. Balancing work-life integration with maintaining productivity is not an easy task, but it's one that needs to be tackled head-on in order to ensure long-term success and satisfaction in both work and life. The consequences of coasting through careers, particularly early on, could have repercussions we're only starting to understand. As the landscape of work continues to evolve, the approach to productivity must evolve with it.

SECTION
TWO
OPERATIONS

14

YOU'LL EVENTUALLY FEEL THE COST OF DISTRACTION

Kane's Considered Analysis

One of the first lectures a marketing student receives at business school is on the three C's—understand your ideal customers, understand your company (capabilities), and understand the competitive landscape. Nailing the three C's allows you, as a marketer, to help a brand or company develop its sustainable competitive advantage, building a moat so wide that it is unassailable by your competitors. Then, once you've established your company's advantage, the key is to scale and build the tallest building in the city. Unfortunately, the business annals are littered with examples of companies that veered from their competitive advantage, became distracted by new, shiny objects, and combusted.

Founded in 1892, the Eastman Kodak Company was the preeminent photographic film company in the world through most of the twentieth century. In fact, as recently as 1976, Kodak held a 90 percent share of film sales in the United States and an 85 percent share of all camera sales in the United States. Even more baffling in hindsight, Kodak developed and patented the first handheld digital camera in 1975. Knowing all of this, how did Kodak lose its enormous advantage in the market? It lost focus.

Fearing its new digital camera business line would threaten its cash cow (photographic film), Kodak began dipping its feet into new verticals that were not aligned with its true capabilities, expanding into pharmaceuticals, memory chips, healthcare imaging, document management, and many others. As digital photography technology progressed, Kodak found itself behind the curve—having not invested in distributing its invention—and spread too thin across verticals into which it had no business dipping its toes. The result? Chapter 11 bankruptcy in 2012.

Over time, customers and the competitive landscape change. Of the three C's, arguably the most important one to get right as a marketer is understanding your company's core competency. With a firm grasp on what it is your company can do better than anybody else, you can navigate changes in the competitive landscape and adjust your service offering to capture new customers. It is absolutely crucial that companies maintain focus or risk pulling out the Jenga piece that topples the entire structure.

James's Unapologetic Outlook

Few things will end up costing you more money than distraction. Well, that technically isn't true. I remember the dot-com bubble and the Chelyabinsk meteor-like crash in 2000 (and also my mild Chipotle habit from *2015 to 2019).

As we write this book, we are experiencing some interesting times in the business world as stocks from some of the world's largest companies tank. While there is a myriad of reasons, from poor products to overhyped business models, many of them simply lost their way.

When the switch is flipped from mission to other things, you begin to walk down paths that rob you of growth, focus, and innovation. This ultimately leads to losses in profit and margin until with an Emeril-like "BAM!" and your stock is down 50 percent. As you walk down these dimly lit tunnels of distraction, you don't see the ending until it's too late. The journey down this tunnel is similar to what happens to the drug cartel in the tunnel as depicted in the movie *Sicario* (If you have seen it, you know; if you haven't seen it, you get the picture). What's the lesson here? Don't walk down paths that get you blasted by a pack of commandos.

When it comes to hyper growth and marketing, you need intense focus to the point where you have tunnel vision and you push away distractions like line-cutters at Disney World. The conversation must always be about the mission, growth, ideas, strategy, and goal. There is no time for anything else. When the conversation goes off track, ask those in the room, "How does this help us achieve the goal?" You don't have to be a bully, but if you don't stand up for the mission, it's only a matter of time before someone leads you awry.

Beyond distractions in the workplace, there is another dangerous distraction. It's like looking at an accident across the street as you go full-on gawker then you yourself end up rear-ending someone. That distraction is expanding into new products, services, or markets before you have dominated your core market.

We like shiny new things because, hey, who doesn't? But when you're trying to grow a company, it is easy to spread yourself thin like the cream cheese on a two-dollar drive-through bagel. You ultimately end up losing on all sides. The reality is, we think by hopping on the new trends we can grow faster. And while this isn't a bad thought, for many, it's a trap they cannot escape. Often, we cannot see the difference between bubbles and things that will last. We chase those bubbles, trying to turn gimmicks into long-term business models. We all know a few companies that have done this, right?

In the end, know this: the distractions of today will be felt months down the road and maybe longer. Everything is going well, then one quarter the numbers come out and you don't know what hit you. Distractions are like radiation poisoning; the damage is done at the time of exposure, but you won't die for days or months down the road. The creeping erosion of mission is our enemy, so keep fighting the good battle and stay focused.

15

DO IT RIGHT OR DON'T DO IT AT ALL (STYLE, WRITING, HANGERS)

James's Realistic Insight

Will the real grammar grouch please stand up? Actually, no, sit your ass back down; no one likes you. I do love word play and lyricism, though, shout out to all of the clever writers out there. There is a difference to me between the nitpickers and the true craftsmen. Anyone can be a sniper, but not everyone can build the rifle.

I don't exactly have a strong handle on the English language (thanks, Mom and Dad), but that's a story for later. When it comes to business and marketing, however, along with a few other topics, I have a lot of insights based on real-life experience. So I have a lot to say, but how I say it and sometimes how I write it comes off a little rough.

One of the keys of doing anything great is knowing what you can and can't do. Once you know that, you must seek out the necessary resources to get the polish done right. For example, I know who I need to proof my content before it is published so they won't take the color out of my creative writing. Much of success at anything comes from understanding what you're not good at, admitting it to yourself, then seeking the resources to get it done right.

The next issue you must face is the "that's good enough" mindset. Every time you see a mattress on the side of the road, you know its journey began with a person tying the ropes and saying, "That's good enough." Most people fall into this category. You must resist the desire to fall into this trap. Anything great, especially in business, isn't easy. The long road is less traveled, but those who took the short route found out it was full of landmines and now it's too late.

You can have *The Elements of Style* on your desk, but if your writing is more boring than an Arctic Circle weather report (I'll save you time—it's always cold), people won't engage with your content. Put the effort in to make it interesting, readable for all levels, while also being aesthetically pleasing. For example, look at Photo 1, which shows the issue of hangers plus top-down \ bottom-top pyramids instead of a squared-up test. I really dislike hangers. If you catch a hanger like Ed Norton in *Rounders*, you know the outcome.

Photo 1 Example of a hanger

If you're not born with it, you must learn to have the most discerning eye on the planet. Then you need the backbone to stand up to your team or consultants and demand they do better. Never settle. If it's not what you envisioned or what you wanted, fight back until you get what you want. If you have to spend all day sorting through 24,000 stock images to get the right one, that is what you have to do. And if you can't find the right image, shoot one so it's done the way you want it.

As you will read in this book multiple times, if you want to win, swimming around the bottom of the lake to feed won't get you much. Everyone is doing the fast, cheap, and easy thing, which works when you want a Costco hot dog. It doesn't work so well when you're trying to grow top-line revenue by double digits. Never settle. It's okay to want perfection when it comes to all things marketing, and to be that person who never takes no for an answer when it comes to your vision.

Kane's Thoughtful Interpretation

I'm a firm believer that the fundamental purpose of writing is to communicate (duh!). The key word in that sentence is "communicate." According to the Flesch–Kincaid scale, Ernest Hemingway wrote at a fourth or fifth grade comprehension level. Regardless of what you feel or believe about his personal politics, it's hard to deny that his writing was beautiful. He communicated well. Think of what he taught so many writers with his four-word story. I've also read my fair share of dense, TLDR-worthy academic papers that generated incredible insight, but were a pain to get through. These are good examples of poor communication. When communication is done well, you feel it somewhere between your neck and your belly button.

As marketers, we're bombarded with enough data, analytics, numbers, ideas, and tactics to fill a twenty-five-hour day. What's been lost, I feel, over the past few years is appreciation for what thoughtful, cutting, and effective copywriting can achieve. It wasn't so long ago that the industrial advertising complex was built on legendary ads that were primarily text driven. If you don't know what I'm talking about, dig up some of the old Nike or VW ads—they're brilliant.

This brings me to my main point—effective communication, regardless of how you do it, is accurate. You cannot achieve extraordinary communication if your vessel is full of holes that need to be patched up the whole way to your destination. In other words, in order to be taken seriously, you have to sweat the small details in your marketing. James's insight on this is 100 percent correct—you must pursue perfection when it comes to your vision for your brand, and marketing is one of the few functions within an organization with the skill set and responsibility to make sure all communications, both internal and external, are done right.

We've all experienced it—scrolling through social media and coming across a brand post (communication) with a typo. What was your immediate response? Did you flinch? Did it stop you in your tracks? What happened to your perception of that brand's credibility in that split second?

We, as human beings, place brands and companies on pedestals. They're more than just agglomerations of human beings. Brands don't have flaws. They inspire. They move markets. They shape societal conversation. Through the products they offer and the brand codes they build around their messaging, companies are larger-than-life constructs. In effect, they're perfection. This is why when we see a brand fall into a typo or a mistake in communications, we flinch. The veil of perfection has been broken, and for most people, another brand can be substituted in—one that hasn't lost its veil of perfection just yet.

As marketers, it is our job to protect our brands and companies from careless errors in communication. The veil of perfection, the greater-than-human qualities that brands exude, are what make brand loyalty possible. Sweat the small things that make this work.

16

YOUR CUSTOMERS AREN'T DUMB

James's Tactical Observation

Did they really think we wouldn't know the food was shrinking? This has happened since the beginning of time. The chip bag seems less full, there's a little less cheese on the pizza, and packages started saying, "Made with mostly real chicken!" Okay, maybe that didn't happen with the chicken, but you get the point.

Shrinkflation is a real thing, and it became an even bigger issue in 2022 as inflation skyrocketed. Companies didn't want to raise prices, so they shrank product. Some even had to do both. I have had to order double chicken, for example, in my burrito in the hope of receiving the normal-sized portion from the past. And maybe, just maybe, you would have caught me ordering two taco entrees because they shrank the food so much, one didn't fill me up anymore. This is only speculation unless someone has photographic proof of me ordering that, though. Pure hearsay, Your Honor!

Now, as consumers, we know the damn thing is shrinking. We are not dumb. In fact, just by way of our own consumption habits, we become experts at certain products. If you eat at the same restaurant four times a week, you likely know the level of their consistency better than the manager does. When it comes to things we consume often, we know the minutia of the products because we are super fans.

From shrinking food to oddball deals, trying to gamify an experience to hide the cost can work to a certain degree, but at what price? Sure you'll get the 20 percent of people who don't care or don't know, but the other 80 percent is on to you. The question is, how far can you push the 80 percent before they don't come back?

Inflation didn't leave companies many options and consumers understand that. My own point of view is, I would rather have what I want than save the $1.10. Now that doesn't work for everyone, especially those on a budget, so this is where you have to create new offerings while still offering what your customers want. They'll just have to pay full freight.

There's a reason restaurant kitchens are often open or have a glass wall. It's a sign of transparency. Many people feel better when they can see what is going on. They don't need to look because they know the glass is there. There is a sense of comfort that someone isn't dropping your chicken on the floor, brushing it off, and throwing it back on your plate. Maybe it's a whole ploy and misdirection, but it's still comforting. Knowing customers aren't dumb, why not find more ways to make them at ease rather than trying to fool them? Give them the glass kitchen experience. Sometimes, it's better to raise the price than to shrink the product, for example. Somehow, paying more for the same amount of food seems better than paying the same old price for less food. Yeah, think about that for a moment...

Kane's Balanced Perspective

It's easy as marketers and operators to chase margin expansion. After all, the better margins you can achieve on your product or service, the more money your business is makes in profits—and who doesn't love profits? Problems arise, however, when corners are cut and practitioners raise prices without providing greater value to the customer.

Why do businesses do this, though? Because it's easy to be fooled into thinking your customers don't know any better. We see this all the time at the grocery store and at the department store. We know we are getting less value for the same amount of money than we did twenty-four months ago, but we make the purchase anyway.

These tactics work for only so long before consumers and—better yet—competitors get wise to them. Every time a business raises prices, it opens up a little bit of a market gap for another company to undercut and grab market share. Then, lo and behold, the original company that got greedy and raised prices to chase better margins—without providing a proportional increase in value—starts to lose its brand equity and customer loyalty, and thus begins a decline into obscurity.

The best way to start growing your margins is to match price increases with some improvement in the efficacy of the product or service, or to add incremental value that signals to the customer that you care. You may be surprised by the market response. Throughout my career as a marketer growing brands and helping companies generate more revenue, I've seen countless cases of better products selling better, even with a substantial price increase. Remember customers are not stupid and will pay for better quality and better value.

The message is clear. Customers won't stand for inauthenticity for long. Don't call yourself a luxury brand if you don't have the quality or heritage to warrant luxury status. Don't chase the high-end consumer when your product or service doesn't provide the requisite features and attributes to appeal to a high-end customer. And by all means don't raise prices for your products or services without a damn good reason to do so. Price reactions to inflation can get you only so far. Add value. Create a better mousetrap. Deliver a better service. Your customers aren't dumb, and your margins will reflect their satisfaction.

17

CASHFLOWIN' LIKE A SPRING RIVER

James's Tenacious Insights

Every business faces this challenge at some point. Often, it's in the early stages of starting the business and the first couple of rapid growth phases. You're getting noticed, the sales are rolling in, but you're lacking the cash flow to hire more people or buy more inventory. So you go to the bank and say "gimme some money" and they basically tell you maybe, after you jump through ninety days of hoops.

But you're not a dog at a show performing fun tricks for the crowd. You're a businessperson trying to do the one fundamental thing you're supposed to do: grow the business. Banks want you to be perfect and entertain them along the way. You'll be questioned about every little detail of your business by someone who has never run a business. It's a sore spot for most entrepreneurs and small business operators. You're sitting there explaining your moves to someone who gets a check from someone else.

Ultimately, they hold the keys to the decision of whether you'll get access to capital or credit to grow your business, which leaves you with coming up with other ideas to keep your company's forward momentum.

Often, people are afraid to negotiate tough terms because they don't want to scare away the client. It's natural to feel that way, and you don't want to make it difficult for them to do business with you. On the other hand, if they want 180-day terms, how can you stay in business?

The truth is, many don't pay on time. Ever. That 180 days has you calling on day 181 asking where your money is. You'll hear excuses: they lost the invoice or didn't get it, the person you were dealing with left the company, you need to update your W-9, you need to fill out the vendor form again, and the list goes on. And on day 210, you call and they stop answering. Finally, you reach out to the CFO asking, "where's my money, man?" like Stewie from *Family Guy*.

And this is if you're lucky. We have had Fortune 100s take over a year to pay a bill that should have been paid Net 30. Next thing you know, you're millions and millions of dollars deep in AR. You don't need the bank. What you need is the clients to pay their damn bills.

Don't be afraid to push for faster payment. Require them to pay by ACH. Email and mail a copy of the invoice. Follow up with them before the due date to ensure they got everything they need. Speak with your attorney and CPA about adding penalty language for late payments or giving a discount for an early payment.

The longer the invoices go unpaid, the greater the chances that you could lose that money due to a customer bankruptcy or it won't get paid at all. Essentially, you need to become a slightly nicer version of Tony

Soprano with a hammer out collecting accounts receivables. Without that cash flow, you can't grow. And, for some, you can't even stay in business.

Kane's Disciplined View

The relationship between cash flow (and free cash flow) and marketing is crucial for small business owners and entrepreneurs to understand because of its importance to the viability of a company. The contentious part of the relationship between cash flow and marketing arises in the difficulty to attribute each and every dollar of marketing spend to a return for the business. There is a well-known saying that "half of all marketing spend is wasted; we just don't know which half," and for many marketers out there, it's true.

Viewed from another lens, however, the relationship between cash flow and marketing is symbiotic. After all, the entire organization is relying on your ability as a marketer to create demand so cash flow can be generated through sales. Without the efforts of marketers, organizations wouldn't function because the revenue would not be there to fund any of the other crucial aspects of the business—human resources, accounting, finance, operations, customer service, and, to some extent, even sales.

This is why marketers shouldn't shy away from conversations around cash flow and profitability. Over my career as a marketer, I have learned that the best management teams are the ones that understand that marketing's value is not in the vanity metrics or tasks that often get associated with the marketing function, but in the challenging work of generating cash flow through demand for the company's products and services.

There is an opportunity, then, for marketers to take on a high-visibility, high-influence role within organizations, especially as it relates to helping create cash flow through sales. One of the areas of insight that marketers have is an understanding of the preferences, demands, and desires of customers out in the real world. These insights form the bed upon which sales teams should then develop the pitches and angles that close sales. Without these insights—that marketers own and can tap into rather easily with the right tools—organizations will struggle on the sales front with disappointing close rates on available leads and prospects.

Many managers think of marketing as a cost center. I won't argue with that. However, the marketing function in your business is a straight line to cash flow. Without marketing, small businesses don't create demand for their products and services, which then means a lack of sales and cash flow. If cash flow is the lifeblood of a business, marketing is the key to providing that lifeblood with the nutrients necessary to survive.

18

PROCESS, WE'RE TALKING ABOUT PROCESS

James's Daring Interpretation

They say to trust the process, which sounds cool and all unless you don't have a process to trust. Now if the process came via a flowchart on a Denny's napkin, that is a whole other issue. See, companies, especially startups and small businesses, often lack processes. Small businesses are sometimes understaffed or cannot attract the right talent. If you have ever been a part of a startup, you know what that chaos looks like. The reality is in both instances, you do the best you can with what you have.

It's something we found interesting over the years at one of our executive search companies. Executives or people in general who came from larger companies with a lot of processes didn't do so well at smaller companies without them. They were used to the rigid way of doing things and doing those things always had "a way." Now you can say that maybe they were the wrong fit, but if they had processes to follow in the first place, they could have figured it out for themselves. Those used to a highly structured environment don't seem to thrive in unstructured ones. The goal here is to become turnkey in the sense that anyone can step into this job and follow the process to success, assuming they have the necessary skill sets to do the job.

That's one good reason to have processes in place, but let's talk about another one. How many times have you filled out a contact form, emailed, or called a business only to never get a call back? Likely a whole hell of a lot. The last time I took count, I received only six calls back out of fifteen businesses I contacted. The time before that, I contacted five architects for a new home design and zero got back to me. It's almost like in this post-COVID day and age, you have to beg people to take your money. Who would have thought stuffing other people's pockets with loot would be so hard? But that's the thing—most of us won't beg anyone to take our money. We will keep calling and emailing until we find someone who wants our business, someone who appreciates our business who also just wants to do good business with a high level of customer service.

There is where you develop a process. We call it business process engineering or, in this case, sales process engineering. How can we design a process that won't fail us or the customer? We start thinking about different ways to poka-yoke a process. Once that is done, it all comes down to training and testing.

For example, how do you make a potential customer feel their experience will be great? First, let the customer know on the website they will get a call or email back within one hour of contacting you. Make sure that phone call goes to a live person every time, either an operator or answering service, who would send that message out to multiple people via email and text. Likewise for email contacts or forms. These systems are tested weekly to make sure everyone is getting the messages. Sometimes, it feels like half of the contact forms on the Internet go nowhere. To top it all off, track the number of weekly inbound messages and match that up with how many people were contacted to ensure the sales team is following the process. This sounds like a lot of work, but once you realize the average customer isn't going to beg you take their money this doesn't sound so bad.

Kane's Structured Opinion

It's a very common idea in management or business building that you're only as good as your processes. Reflecting on this, the sentiment is probably truer and more important than I've given it credit for over the years, especially when thinking about how important processes can be across so many different organizational functions.

To a marketer, process can sometimes feel a bit stifling, at least when it comes to creativity. To get good at anything, you need processes to drive performance, but more importantly, to drive your learning and insights. What do I mean by this? You need consistency in the way you do things in business so that you can establish benchmarks with which to judge performance. With these benchmarks, you can work on getting better. It's the only way.

I heard an excellent analogy on a podcast recently—which I'll paraphrase and tweak a little bit for this chapter. Goals and targets in business are like the address you put into the GPS in your car. You get in your car, plug in the address of where you want to go, and that's the start. What happens if you stop there? You don't go anywhere. You're still sitting in the car, idle, looking at the GPS.

You need to drive the car. This is what process is like in business. Processes are the guardrails that allow you to make progress toward your destination. Without processes—methods and practices with which you do everything consistently everyday—you end up in chaos. Chaos is troublesome in business, especially in small business environments where you are handling nearly everything on your own, wearing many different hats. Chaos, while fun, can be deceiving because chaos can feel like progress. Chaos can feel like you're doing work. But that's the problem with operating without processes—work will always find a way to fill your day as a small business owner. There will always be another fire to put out. But processes allow you to map out what you need to do to ensure you are consistently moving in the right direction.

Chaos is also trouble in small business when you're delivering products or services to customers. Customers hate chaos. Think of the last time you bought something from a company that was relatively new and still working things out on the back end. I can think of a time when a brand owner forgot to ship my order and then reasoned it out as a fault in their systems on the back end. Chaos is not fun for a customer. Processes protect you, as a small business owner, from skipping steps and letting things fall through the cracks. Whenever you set up a thoughtful process, you build quality control for your business. It's always a good idea.

19

CANNIBALIZING SALES FOR MARKET DOMINANCE

James's Raw Point of View

If you haven't received the message yet, we are trying to teach you how to take over the world here. We never step into the arena thinking we will lose or barely win. In the business world, a win isn't a win unless it's complete dominance—that is how you have to think to succeed. If you're not thinking that way, someone else is, and they are looking to take your lunch money.

I wrote a paper once that was a little different than what the professor was looking for. The case study was about closing stores because they were not as profitable as they should be, because of close proximity to each other. Well, my paper was on how you have to cannibalize sales if you ever want to dominate the market. The professor reached out to me to discuss as they never had anyone write something like this before. We chatted for quite some time about this strategy and why it made so much sense to me. My explanation was simple: if you have the ability to suck enough oxygen from the market that your competitors can't breathe, do it.

Let's use Starbucks in NYC as an example. In Manhattan, people say there is a Starbucks on every corner. In some cases, based on the walking patterns of pedestrians, maybe some of these Starbucks branches are too close to each other. The store in the middle is therefore siphoning off sales from the other stores around it. Do you close the middle store?

I say no, and this is why. If Starbucks has saturated the coffee market to the point that its average sales dip a bit across a few stores, there is likely no room for any other coffee joint unless it is unique. Store profitability drops, which could be an issue if you own a franchise, but in a case where all stores are corporately owned, not so much. You could also make the case that Wall Street will care if you're a public company and they are eyeballing profits, so that pressure may cause you to make different decisions as well. If I own a giant chain like this, I will lose a little profit to make sure I own the market. I always like to think of it the way drug dealers do. Once you own this corner, it's your corner, and you're not giving it up without a lot of shell casings hitting the ground.

During the industrial revolution, this is the mentality everyone had about business; maybe we have just gone a little soft in the modern world. Once you understand someone is always coming after you, you have no choice but to figure out a way to stay alive. Most companies weren't meant to stay in business forever, but we want to stick around for as long as we can. We know how high the failure rate is for startups, and just getting to that five-year mark is very difficult. If you stay on your toes and wake up every morning thinking marketing dominance, you give yourself better odds to succeed.

Kane's Methodical Analysis

Business school students take marketing and strategy courses that teach that business owners need to be aware of cannibalization of sales, because the thinner you spread your sales over increasing capital expenditures, the less profitable each location ends up being. While this makes total sense for organizations that operate with franchise models (you don't want to anger your franchisees by chopping into their demand with new stores too close to one another), I've always enjoyed James's take on cannibalization from the standpoint of sucking all the oxygen out of the market. At the end of the day, every piece of real estate your company takes up is real estate a competitor cannot occupy.

It's important, though, as marketers, to always be thinking of the new iteration of your product or service that will put your existing product or service out of business. If you're not doing this, rest assured your competitors are. Some of the most high-value insights you can bring to an organization are the ones that allow the business to take a step into the future. Is there room for your small business's products to expand into new markets? If launching new products eats into your existing sales but allows your organization to fortify its moat, that's a decision you need to explore.

The reality is that for a small business owner, cannibalization should not be a top-of-mind concern. Between James's market dominance perspective and my perspective of ensuring you are always propelling your company into the future, establishing new locations, putting new products and services into the market that chip into existing sales but expand your company's customer base and allow you to grow revenue is a good idea.

So shift your perspective on cannibalization as a bad thing and think of it as a way of future-proofing your business. We are currently working with a client to build a service that will inevitably make a million-dollar-a-year business line redundant, but the new lower-cost, larger-margin service will generate more profitable revenue, expand market share, and establish a closer bond with customers through a higher-value experience. We are not afraid to go down this path with this client because we are future-proofing the business. An investment today in a bigger, better business tomorrow is always a good idea.

20

WHITE-GLOVING ALL TOUCH POINTS

Kane's Measured Standpoint

You know that saying, "You never get a second chance to make a first impression"? For businesses, especially small ones, every interaction a customer has with their brand is a chance to make a first impression. These interactions, or "touch points," are potential moments of truth where the business gets a shot at impressing the customer. Each touch point is an opportunity to win over a customer, deepen their loyalty, or turn a casual browser into a dedicated advocate. And it's through the concept of white-gloving all touch points that you can ensure these opportunities are not wasted.

White-gloving, a term born from the high standards of luxury hotels and concierge services, refers to the meticulous attention to detail and personalized service that create a seamless and superior customer experience. Translated to a business context, it means examining every single touch point—from browsing your website, speaking to a sales rep, to unwrapping the product—and ensuring the customer experiences nothing less than excellence.

The first step in white-gloving all touch points is to map out your customers' journey. What are the potential interactions they can have with your business? These may include your website, social media platforms, customer service lines, storefronts, and even indirect interactions such as online reviews and word-of-mouth referrals. This map should cover all stages of the customer life cycle, from initial discovery to post-purchase support.

Once you've identified all potential touch points, examine each one closely. Is your website easy to navigate, with clear information about your products or services? Are your customer service representatives trained and empowered to resolve issues and answer queries effectively? Is your product packaging inviting and reflective of your brand? Are the conditions of your physical store conducive to a pleasant shopping experience?

Remember white-gloving isn't just about doing things right. It's about going above and beyond to make the customer's experience remarkable. You're not just answering a customer query; you're providing valuable advice or getting back to them faster than anybody else. You're not just delivering a product. You're creating an experience.

Investing in white-gloving all touch points may seem daunting, particularly for small businesses operating on tight budgets. However, the ROI on creating an exceptional customer experience is undeniable. Customers today are spoilt for choice, and what often makes them choose one business over another isn't just the product, but the overall experience.

White-gloving all touch points not only attracts new customers but also builds loyalty among existing ones. It turns customers into brand advocates who will promote your business to their networks. It builds a positive reputation that acts as a powerful marketing tool.

Finally, remember white-gloving is not a one-time project. It requires continuous monitoring, reviewing, and refining. Always be on the lookout for ways to improve, and be receptive to feedback from your customers. After all, they're the ones you're doing this for.

Every touch point matters. By committing to a white-glove approach at every interaction, you're setting your business apart, creating memorable experiences, and building lasting relationships with your customers. When you treat every touch point as an opportunity to impress, you'll find that your business isn't just providing a product or service—it's delivering excellence.

James's Edgy Take

Sometimes my mind goes to strange places when I'm writing books. The title for this chapter was based on how we built several of our own multi-million-dollar companies.

We've learned over the years that, by the time you get up to six, seven, or eight-plus brands, everyone is fighting at the bottom. Most of these people are competing on price, giving the product or service away and losing money, just as a loss leader. Such businesses usually offer fast and cheap products or services, but provide low quality and poor customer service. We've always chosen to go where the air is thinner because we can fly up there. We compete at the higher level. That means white-gloving all customer touch points.

Now, when I say my mind goes to a strange place, it makes me think of books I've read and interviews I've watched about picking up on people's habits. People will leave traces of themselves based on the things they say and do. So my crazy, abstract thought imagines a crime scene where you're leaving DNA all over the place. At the end of the day, the CSI people are going to pick up on all of this while you thought you were going to get away with it.

You'll most likely experience this within restaurants and other providers of hospitality services. Maybe you're at a restaurant and the waiter brings out a chipped wine glass or decanter. To them, it's not a big deal, and they may think the customer is too stupid to notice. To me, on the other hand, this is a little piece of the DNA left behind at the crime scene. If you're willing to bring me a chipped wine glass or a chipped decanter, I have to start questioning what else is going on in the back of the house that I can't see. These are all those little traces that the customer does pick up on. Maybe the company doesn't care or that particular employee at that moment doesn't care, but the customer certainly cares.

You can also experience this when dealing with products and services far beyond the hospitality industry. For example, if I call a company and it takes two days for them to call me back, I'm already getting the feeling that they are not very customer centric. Let's chalk that up as one little drop of blood left on the mirror somewhere. It's not enough to prove a murder happened, but you'll certainly remember it.

Finally, a sales rep calls you back and the call goes okay. They promise to send you an email to recap what you're looking for and say you can respond with any questions. You get the email, you send back a couple of questions, and it takes the sales rep another couple of days to get back to you. So now we have found blood splattered on the floor. The sales rep finally gets back to you, but the email is short with grammatical errors, and they didn't answer all of your questions. We officially have a crime scene.

We leave little hints (DNA) throughout the process about how we feel about customer service or when we make mistakes. You have to remember the customer is keeping track of all this. I use hospitality or restaurants as a primary example as it's the easiest way to display it. How many times have you been seated at a restaurant and it's taken fifteen minutes to get your drink order? Then it takes forty-five minutes for your food to come out, and some of it's not done right. Then while you're waiting for the dessert menu, the server pulls the oh-so-common disappearing server act. They disappear for fifteen or twenty minutes, and no one knows where they went.

You typically won't see this in very high-end restaurants. Hell, at some high-end restaurants you end up with two servers, one who is running drinks and all the extras plus one who is managing the food order. This is a high level of customer service. This is white-gloving the entire customer experience.

So instead of leaving little traces of DNA everywhere as you make mistakes in delivering the customer experience, why not look for ways to make sure every single touch point is well received from the customer? The biggest trick here is getting employees who care. This is one thing you're never going to fix. If an employee doesn't care, there's nothing you can do—no process, no incentive, nothing—that will make this a white-glove experience.

We live by some simple rules. If someone calls one of our companies, we always promise to call back within one hour. If you email us or text us, it's the same response. We always do what we say we're going to do, and we do it when we say we were going to do it. Always kill customers with kindness, no matter how difficult they are. When you face customers, be well-groomed, well-dressed, and well-spoken at all times regardless if you're in person or on a Zoom call.

It's not that hard. It's that old mantra of under-promise and over-deliver. You don't need the customers to experience customer delight, but you want them to be pretty damn close. You never want to give them a reason to shop around and go somewhere else. Every touch point should matter regardless of how simple it seems to you.

21

WEAPONIZING YOUR SALES TEAM

James's Provocative Understanding

Napoleon said, "Bring me the lucky generals." We say, "Bring us the sales-people willing to pound the phones and create their own luck." We always look at the sales department as having its own personal stash of ICBMs that we can dispatch at will and completely take out a competitor.

Since about 2010, most companies have gone after a fully digital strategy, believing that's all they need to generate sales and rapidly grow. That works well when you have a viral or trending product and everybody wants it, but it doesn't work so well if you're a legacy business fighting for market share.

Some of our best clients across any one of my companies have come from picking up the phone and dialing until we found someone who needed our service and valued what we had to offer. See, that's the issue with pursuing an all-digital strategy. It's kind of like going to a bar with ten guys for every girl. All ten guys are competing for the girl and only one can win. Hell, maybe no guys win in this one.

That's digital for you. When someone needs your product or service, they jump into a search engine, do a search, then look at the first three or four or five results and possibly a couple of the ads at the top. Next thing you know, they're talking to seven different companies.

Now, you don't have to be a mathematician here, but how do you like the odds of being one in seven? That's worse than casino odds. You may as well play blackjack or baccarat. If you're feeling really lucky, why not just bet it all on black on the roulette wheel? You have a greater chance of winning than you do of winning the one-out-of-seven deal.

That's why I've always been hyper-focused when I'm building sales teams. I like putting myself in the position to be one of one. Sure, sometimes you get someone interested or you catch them at the right time, when they have a need and they're going to cross-shop. But if you were there first and you spent the time to develop and foster a relationship and some kind of rapport, there's a high chance you'll win regardless of them looking at other bids.

The amount of money people spend on SEO and organic searches, factored in with how much they spend on AdWords and other social ads, is actually pretty crazy when you look at it. Let's say you're spending $500,000 a year on AdWords, SEO, and other social media. You could have a sales team that is five- to seven-people deep, that is strategically targeting the ideal customer base, that is going to help you grow and likely net you higher-yielding deals.

Now, why do I say higher-yielding deals? This is something we learned from an all-digital strategy. When a prospective customer jumps into

Google and they end up calling five, six, seven, or even ten different companies, all of a sudden, it becomes a battle about price. When you have that many options, you can typically get what you want at the price you want. So, over the years, we have found that leads generated from purely online methods typically have a lower profit margin than the things we hunted for ourselves.

The other benefit of a sales team is weaponizing it. The fact that you can go to war with a particular competitor if they've been eating away at your business is paramount. If you know a particular competitor has been stealing a lot of your Chicago business through digital platforms, and you want to take back some of that market share, you can now hyper focus on that location and get to those sales before they even enter a Google search.

It's an aggressive way of thinking, but this is how we think because we think the win. We always say if you're going to meet us on the field of battle, expect helmet-to-helmet contact. This is a competition and we are here to win. Technology has made it very easy for people to get lazy and complacent. Pop in some AI-generated ad content and throw some ad budget behind it and watch your company grow. Technically, this works until too many people are fighting for that same digital space. Our lesson here is, fewer and fewer people are picking up the phone in order to do real sales, which creates a limitless opportunity. Right now, if you're serious about growth and tired of worrying about whether Google changes your rankings and how that's going to affect your business, we suggest you build a sales team and weaponize it to take back your market share.

Kane's Calculated Opinion

It comes as no surprise that in today's digital-first environment, many companies are enamored with online marketing and social media. These platforms offer unprecedented reach, low costs, and instant gratification in the form of vanity metrics. However, in this rush to digitize, the power of direct, personal, and engaged sales teams is often overlooked. This is particularly true for small businesses, which are typically more cash-strapped and resource-poor compared to their larger counterparts. But let me let you in on a secret—a well-equipped, determined, and resourced sales team can be one of the most potent weapons in your business arsenal.

Let me use a military metaphor. While your competitors are launching blanket airstrikes with their digital strategies, hoping to hit something valuable, you could be performing precision strikes, targeting customers with pinpoint accuracy through a personalized, hands-on approach. The difference is that with the latter approach, you are conducting the business equivalent of hand-to-hand combat: cold-calling sales and making valuable connections. It's intimate, it's direct, and, when done right, it's incredibly effective.

The initial step to weaponizing your sales team is to make the necessary investment. This means not only hiring competent salespeople but also ensuring they have the tools, training, and resources they need to succeed. Equip them with a deep understanding of your products or services, customer needs, market dynamics, and competition. Teach them not only to sell but to solve problems, build relationships, and provide unparalleled value. Remember, in this form of combat, their words are their ammunition and their understanding is their armor.

While investment in a sales team may seem significant, especially when compared to some digital strategies, it's important to understand that the ROI can be immense. A successful sales team can bring in not only revenue but also valuable market insights, loyal customers, and strategic relationships. They can help you understand your customers' needs, desires, and pain points better than any online survey. Plus, their victories, much like a weapon's successful deployment, can have a psychological impact on your team, boosting morale and fostering a culture of success.

Second, utilize the benefits of your size. As a small business owner, you can leverage your company's agility and flexibility to offer personalized experiences and build deeper relationships. Your sales team can engage in meaningful conversations, respond to concerns promptly, and offer solutions larger, more bureaucratic organizations can't match. In this era of automation and depersonalization, the human touch is not just refreshing—it's a potent weapon. A digital-first strategy isn't as responsive to changing market conditions, because you are at the mercy of the search engine algorithms and the intent of the potential lead.

Last, a crucial but often overlooked aspect is building a supportive, rewarding, and motivating culture within your sales team. They are on the front lines, often facing rejections, tackling challenges, and exploring new territories. They need to know their efforts are valued, their victories are celebrated, and their development is prioritized. Much like soldiers on a battlefield, they need to believe in the cause, trust their leadership, and feel supported by their comrades.

While digital strategies and social media have their place in today's business world, don't underestimate the power of a well-equipped, motivated, and supported sales team. It might require a substantial investment and a different mindset, but the potential rewards are immense. With the right approach, your sales team can be more than just a revenue generator; they can be your business's most powerful weapon, capable of securing victory in the competitive battlefield of the market.

22
PARIS SYNDROME & HIRING

James's Dynamic Stand

Have you ever gotten so excited for something you couldn't sleep? Okay, sure, as kids or, hell, maybe even as adults, we find this often happens the night before Christmas. But have you ever done that, let's say, about a future dining experience, a date, or a place you always wanted to visit? There is a phenomenon called Paris syndrome I have always found interesting. It's happened to me several times.

Paris syndrome is essentially extreme disappointment at seeing what Paris really is versus what you thought Paris was. We have all experienced that when traveling, and social media doesn't make it any better. Between the perfect photos with no crowds, filters, and blue checkmarks for perceived authority, you get overhyped for something that on any other day may be average.

You have also likely experienced this when dating. You spent time getting to know someone you hadn't met yet in person. Maybe it was writing emails back and forth, talking on the phone, or, in this day and age, texting and creeping on their social media. In your mind, you develop this idea of who they are, and you even begin to develop an image of who they will be when you finally meet them.

Then you meet them, and they don't look like their profile pic, nor do they seem as smart or funny as you expected. Somewhere between the hype and excitement for something new, you also created this image in your head of who you wanted them to be, which they are not, only to leave you extremely disappointed.

What does all of this have to do with hiring? This exact thing happens when you're hiring, and let's not make this mistake as the costs are pretty damn high. Not only does this happen during the hiring process, it's even more complicated. We can get super hyped when we see a good résumé, have a good interview, and start to think about how this person will help change the company. Now your mind starts creating this vision of what you want them to be, which doesn't always match up with who they are.

To go with that, do you really know who they are? Let me use another dating reference. Everyone shows up to a first date showered, with a fresh haircut, well groomed and dressed, and usually on their best behavior. Now, for some couples, by date six, they're chilling in sweatpants and asking themselves: is this the same person I met a few weeks ago?

The same damn thing happens during the interview and hiring process. Someone you thought was a highly punctual, driven, motivated go-getter sometimes ends up being the perpetually late employee who keeps talking about work-life balance while working a thirty-two-hour week.

This is why we often say be "slow to hire" and make sure you follow your hiring process. Don't become low-key over someone who hasn't proven themselves yet, and never get emotional. Let's not forget you're often dealing with over-embellished résumés that are now even more enhanced with AI writing them. Everyone shows up to the interview saying they can do the job without even blinking. Those AI résumés often include bullets about accomplishments someone else did at the candidate's prior job.

So, during the interview, you're getting the first date image and you're sold. If you don't keep a level head throughout the hiring process, you're going to end up very disappointed later when this person isn't who you thought they would be. My biggest takeaway in hiring—maybe in life—is this: don't allow your mind to create an image of what you want someone to be. It never works.

Kane's Logical View

When it comes to business truths, here's one you can bank on: hiring is not for the fainthearted. Whether your corporation is a budding startup or a flourishing small business, this adage rings true. Hiring involves navigating a labyrinth of complex human dynamics and decisions, all while trying to forecast future needs and keep your company culture intact.

Paris syndrome is a strangely fitting analogy for the hiring conundrum. This unusual psychological affliction strikes tourists who arrive in Paris expecting a constant reel of postcard-worthy scenes only to encounter the city's grittier realities. Reality doesn't meet expectation.

Now let's apply this concept to hiring. As employers, we can sometimes don rose-tinted glasses, envisioning the perfect candidate who will magically solve all our business woes. However, just like the disillusioned tourist realizing the Eiffel Tower isn't visible from every Parisian café, we find our picture-perfect hire doesn't exist in the flesh.

There's a certain allure to scaling up a team rapidly. A bustling workspace, the dynamic chatter of ideas, and the sense of collective purpose can be seductive. They feel like signs of momentum, of the business going places. But, like the tourist succumbing to Paris syndrome, we soon discover a larger team doesn't equate to enhanced productivity or a better business. In fact, dealing with the whims and motivations of other human beings can be the biggest stress a manager can face. So how do we, as small business owners, avoid falling prey to our own version of Paris syndrome when hiring?

First, the hiring process calls for clear, grounded expectations. We must recognize no employee, however talented, is a business panacea. Instead of casting a wide net for a jack-of-all-trades, concentrate on defining the precise needs for the specific role you are looking to fill.

Second, hiring demands patience. It is an investment of time and energy that shouldn't be rushed. Every interview, every conversation, is an opportunity to understand more about the candidate's values, passions, and cultural fit. Remember you are dealing with complex individuals, not commodities.

Last, bear in mind that hiring is a two-way street. While you are assessing potential employees, they are evaluating you and your business. It's essential to portray an accurate picture of your company and its culture, ensuring it's a place where potential hires can envision their future growth.

Avoiding Paris syndrome in the hiring process doesn't mean compromising on the quality of candidates. Rather, it's about approaching the process with a grounded mindset: realistic about candidates' abilities, patient in the search for the right fit, and attentive to the mutual compatibility between the employee and the business.

Much like the seasoned traveler who appreciates Paris for its eclectic blend of charm and chaos, smart business owners realize successful hiring is a deliberate, measured process. It's not a mad sprint toward an illusion of perfection, but a thoughtful marathon in the pursuit of long-term business health and growth.

23

EVER EXPANDING LIKE MY WAISTLINE

James's Blunt Assessment

This is another abstract thought I had while traveling. When I was grow-ing up in Michigan, it always seemed like everyone went up north—they didn't go anywhere else. If they did, it was typically Florida. I never heard about anyone visiting Europe or California, but that could be because I grew up in a lower-middle-class area. Overall, as I got older, I did notice Michigan people often stayed in their bubble.

Now, that doesn't mean Michiganders don't travel anywhere; that would be silly to think. Funnily enough, though, recently, I read a survey that ranked states based on how much of the population stays in their home state for life. Michigan ranked forty-seventh. This wasn't surprising if you grew up in Michigan.

I'm going to go back to my earlier comment about Florida. Even right now, I'm thinking about how many people I know in Michigan who were in Florida in the past twelve months, and it's a lot. Not only do they vacation in Florida; I'm thinking about how many people I know who have a second home there. Not Hilton Head in South Carolina, not Texas, not California, and certainly nothing out west in the mountains. It's Florida.

See, if I go to Florida, I go to Miami. South Beach is lively, the pool at the W is a blast, and the restaurant scene down there is great. I come across mostly people from the East Coast or Europe when I'm in Miami, not many people from Michigan. So, if Michiganders go to Florida often, and they are not in Miami, where do they go exactly? Well, if they're not in Orlando for Disney World, which let's say that one doesn't count, they are in the Tampa area, down to Fort Myers, and, if they're of retirement age and wealthy, even down by Naples.

When I talk about Miami, people in Michigan look at me like I'm crazy. When they tell me about the west coast of Florida, I look at them like they're crazy. As I was telling somebody one day about these travel patterns, they cut me off and said, "I see more Michigan people that I know in Tampa than I do when I'm home in Michigan."

As I'm processing all of this, I'm thinking that if I ever plan on expanding a restaurant or retail concept outside the state of Michigan, the first place I would probably go is Tampa. I already have a built-in audience of like-minded people there, and I have them in masses. When I say like-minded people, I meant that, if that is where Michiganders tend to congregate, you'd have to assume that people in the area have very similar tastes to them. It's almost like the research is done for you at this point.

If I didn't have these data points upfront, how hard would they be to find? Well, they wouldn't be that hard to find if I just looked up the busiest routes from one airport to another. I already have my answer. That's the simple trick—just look up the most common flight paths and density!

I'm not likely to see a large number of airplanes flying from Detroit to Pittsburgh, for example. That doesn't mean I would never consider opening something in Pittsburgh; it's just that if I'm going to expand outside of Michigan, Pittsburgh probably wouldn't be my first choice. In the same way, if you don't see tremendous crowds of people from New York City going to Tampa but they do go to Miami, it would make more sense to open a New York City expansion in Miami. It is funny to say that because I was just in South Beach, and the New York influence down there from Italian restaurants to NYC-style pizza was huge. Hell, even my Uber driver said he grew up in Little Italy in New York and moved down to South Beach about twenty-five years ago.

We've witnessed a lot of people make mistakes when expanding their businesses. You think you start with your local metro area where your reputation has been built and you're going to slowly grow outward from there. It seems easy enough, but that's usually not how it goes. Often what happens is, someone from another state comes and wants to buy a territory for their own home state and then, the next thing you know, you're opening franchises 1,500 miles away. But I'm going to go back to that way of thinking if I'm in Michigan: am I better off opening my first location in Cleveland, or should I go somewhere like Tampa?

It's easy to get caught up in the local idea when Cleveland is only three hours away. In a strange way, though, Tampa may have more Michigan people and more Michigan-like people than does Cleveland itself.

Another way to look at it is opening up in major travel hubs. When Effen vodka first came to the States, we couldn't get it in Michigan. Effen had a black cherry vodka I wanted for my cocktail bar at home. This was back when liquor wasn't shipped that easily. But the vodka was available in New York, and obviously New York is a heavy global travel destination. So, if I wanted Effen black cherry vodka, I had to bring a couple of bottles back with me from New York. It wouldn't have made much sense for Effen to open up shop in Jackson, Mississippi, first.

The lesson of the story is that, when you're expanding early on, it's very important to go where you already have a built-in audience. It's easy to get caught up in the excitement of growth and thinking everybody wants your product or service. In reality, that's not true. Some things will work in one state but they won't work two states over.

So, is it as easy as looking at the most common plane routes? Maybe it's not that easy, but in this day and age, when we have so much data at our fingertips, that first part of expansion should be a little bit easier if you find clever ways to use the data.

Kane's Careful Consideration

Every entrepreneur dreams of scaling up. Your brand name spread across the city, the country, or even the globe is a vision that fuels late nights and early mornings. But expansion, my friend, is a tricky beast. It isn't about sprouting branches all over the place just because it looks good on paper. Rather, it's about mindful growth—knowing who you're growing for and why. Let's dig deeper.

Expanding your small business successfully rests on the bedrock of three understandings: your value proposition, your customers' motivations, and your target demographic. Miss one, and your expansion could turn into an overreach.

First up is your value proposition. This is the heart of your business—the unique mix of product, service, quality, and price that you offer. It's what sets you apart from the competition. Without a well-defined value proposition, your business is just another face in the crowd. The key to expansion is to double down on this unique value, not dilute it. You don't want to grow at the expense of what made your business special in the first place. Expansion must enhance your value proposition, not erode it.

Second is understanding why people buy your product or service. People don't just buy what you sell; they buy why you sell it. They are moved by the story behind your product, the mission of your company, and how your offerings make them feel. Expansion mustn't tarnish this "why." As you grow your business, remember to infuse every new branch with the ethos and story your customers have come to love.

Now comes the last but equally crucial piece of the puzzle—your exact demographic. One of the common pitfalls in business expansion is the temptation to target everyone, which results in targeting no one effectively. Instead, identify your demographic with laser-like precision. Understand its habits, preferences, and pain points. Get to know it so well you can anticipate its needs.

This level of granularity might seem excessive, but it pays off. When you know who your core customers are, you can focus your expansion efforts to serve them better. You can tailor your marketing strategies, fine-tune your products, and even select new business locations based on this understanding. A well-defined demographic becomes a compass guiding your growth in the right direction.

Let me be clear—expansion is not about vanity. Sure, rapid growth might make for good headlines and impressive investor presentations, but superficial expansion can be a business's downfall. We've all seen companies overextend themselves, diluting their brand value and stretching their resources too thin. This approach might generate short-term buzz, but it often leads to long-term difficulties.

Instead, think of expansion as a strategic move to better serve your customers and enhance your value proposition. Let your understanding of your customers and their needs be the guiding light leading you toward the right opportunities. Expansion should not be an aim in itself, but a means to deliver more value to more people.

As you dream of scaling your business, remember meaningful expansion requires a deep understanding of your value proposition, your customers, and your target demographic. Expansion isn't about being bigger; it's about being better. So, as you prepare for this exciting phase, get granular about your demographic, maintain your unique value, and keep your customers' motivations at the heart of all your decisions. That way, you're sure to expand in a way that's sustainable, profitable, and true to your brand's ethos.

24

THESE PRICES ARE TOO DAMN HIGH

James's Intrepid Viewpoint

I have been thinking back to some of the superior parenting moments of my mother and father for the limited time they were around the house. Kurt Russell starred in a movie called *Used Cars* that my father probably had on VHS tape, or maybe we watched it on TV. Now, that movie came out in 1980, so I remember watching it when I was a child, probably eight or nine years old, a few years after it was released. I'll save some of those childhood stories for my other book as my childhood was pretty wild.

In that movie, salesmen from a couple of car dealerships fought each other. There was a scene I never forgot. The salesmen were blowing up cars on a lot of a competing dealer live on TV. One of the lines is "that price is too f*cking high!" and then they blow the car up on TV. For the rest of my life, every time I see a ridiculous price, especially in this post-COVID era, I have had this sound in my head going "that's too f*cking high, BOOM."

For example, if I get a sandwich from a chain these days, it's probably twelve to fourteen dollars and I'm still hungry afterward. The bread seems smaller and someone back at corporate thought it was funny to play "hide the meat" with the customers. You have a chicken sandwich and it hardly has any chicken on it. It's so bad, I don't understand how they get away with it. And that's the thing about pricing. When your prices are too high, you might get away with it once or twice, and then the customer stops coming back. I'm now at that point. I really like that sandwich, but I feel ripped off.

Another chain I loved started doing the same thing during COVID. At both of those places, I find myself having to spend more money on "double meat." At times, it seems like I'm paying for double meat in order to get the original portion. I went from eating at these places three to four times a week, sometimes more, to not going at all because the price for the smaller portion is just too high.

Value is a funny thing, and it's always in the eye of the beholder. As many times as I've been at a steakhouse sawing on a $200 tomahawk ribeye, I've also seen a mac and cheese with black truffles for $40. When it's going on the expense account, no one's complaining about the $40 truffle mac and cheese. Many of us enjoy it because we love the taste of black truffles. On the other hand, some people would think that's a rip-off. Pricing is strange because it is so subjective.

High pricing often comes down to how we perceive value. We wouldn't complain about the high pricing if there was so much meat in there we couldn't finish it all. You have to make the decision: mathematically, can you offer this product or service at a reasonable price or not? Maybe you're better off just adding more chicken and upping the price a little more.

This is likely why shrinkflation went along with higher prices post COVID. When managers of companies in the food industry looked at where their food costs should be plus their labor costs, they probably had no choice but to shrink portions and raise prices. It's a terrible spot to be in in the business world and it is understandable, but the consumer doesn't care. The other issue is food costs have come down, but prices have not come down at restaurants yet. With so many options out there now, consumers don't have to go to the same chains anymore. Lately, I found myself going to the local deli where a sandwich still costs fifteen dollars, but it's actually two whole sandwiches I can barely finish. This goes back to how we perceive value. To me, this sandwich is a better value and just as tasty, and it comes from a locally owned business.

Last, I want to touch on a concept I have been talking about for maybe the past ten years. It's how we see money and the value of money. Let's use Little Caesars as an example. When Little Caesars's pizza is five dollars, that seems like a pretty good deal, and no one ever complains. If the price increased to six or seven dollars or even eight dollars, people probably wouldn't say too much. But at ten dollars, people would begin to say it's not worth it.

Here's the crazy thing. Even if the cost of the pizza doubled from five dollars to ten and all wages in the country doubled as well, your mind would still get stuck on the fact that that five-dollar Little Caesars pizza now costs ten dollars. Now you begin to think, "Well, instead of spending ten dollars on Little Caesars, I'd rather spend fourteen on a Jet's pizza." The same issue may happen with Subway as well. If it gets to the point that Subway costs ten to twelve dollars, you may spend a few dollars more and go to Jersey Mike's or Penn Station instead.

Those on a tight budget obviously are always going to choose the cheapest option regardless. We've learned post-COVID that people are willing to spend more money for things that are a little better or have a slightly higher perceived value. But the consumer has less tolerance for rising prices while at the same time receiving less.

Pricing is a magical thing. If you have something everybody wants and they're going to line up at the door to get it, you have nothing to worry about. But if you're selling sandwiches and your customers are still hungry after eating one, well, there's ten sandwich shops within a mile radius so you probably have a problem. Maybe things will change in the coming years, but right now, things just don't make sense in the economy. But, if you want to survive, you have to find creative ways to keep your prices in line and your consumers happy while things eventually normalize (we hope).

Kane's Studied Perspective

Set foot in any university's business school, and you will likely be bombarded with theories, models, and strategies for pricing. From cost-plus to value-based pricing, the academic world has a plethora of approaches to selling your product at the right price point. Business schools make it seem so straightforward, as if you just plug in some numbers, follow the formula, and, voila, you have your perfect price. But, as with many things, reality is often more complex, more volatile, and, frankly, more unpredictable.

Pricing isn't just an exercise in mathematics or economics. It's a dance with human behavior and perception. As entrepreneurs, we may understand our costs and have a firm grasp on the value our products offer, but we are often blindsided by how our customers perceive this value. How many times have you heard or perhaps yourself said, "The price is too high"? That statement isn't always about the actual price. It's about the perceived value in relation to the price.

Let's delve into an example. In an inflationary environment, the costs of running a business naturally rise. Whether it's raw materials, labor, transportation, or other overhead expenses, everything seems to be getting more expensive. As a business owner, you have a few choices. You can cut costs elsewhere (often compromising quality or service), you can absorb the costs and see your margins shrink, or you can pass the costs on to the consumer.

Passing the cost on to the consumer seems like the most logical option. After all, shouldn't the customer bear the burden of the increase in costs? In theory, yes, but in practice, it's not that straightforward. Enter the laws of supply and demand. As prices go up, demand often goes down, especially if consumers perceive the price as too high, regardless of the reasons behind the increase.

Herein lies the complexity of pricing in the real world. A product or service might be priced perfectly according to business school theory, yet still be met with resistance from consumers who perceive it as too expensive. This perception isn't necessarily linked to the actual value of the product or the cost of its production. It's influenced by a multitude of factors, many of which are outside of your control, such as the state of the economy, competition, and customer sentiment.

So what's an entrepreneur to do? First, recognize pricing is not a "set it and forget it" process. It requires constant evaluation and adjustment. Second, be transparent. If prices must rise due to increased costs, communicate this to customers. Consumers are more understanding when they know the "why" behind a price increase. Finally, focus on delivering exceptional value. When customers believe they are receiving more value than what they're paying for, price becomes a smaller part of their purchasing decision.

In the end, pricing will always be a balancing act between covering costs, making a profit, and satisfying customers. It's a dance that can feel clumsy at times, but with practice and a deep understanding of your market, you can keep your customers happily dancing along with you.

25

THAI, SUSHI, KOREAN BBQ, CHINESE

James's Unyielding View

You always see restaurants around the neighborhood, and they never seem to make it very long. In the window, a sign will say: Thai food, Chinese, sushi, and Korean BBQ. It leaves you thinking, "What the hell is it you actually do well?" More than likely, none of it is good.

Typically, if I want good Korean BBQ, it's going to come from a place that does only Korean BBQ. If I want the best Chinese food, it usually comes from a place that focuses on Chinese food, like the joint not too far from where I grew up. You see where I'm going with this.

If these restaurateurs are lucky, they stay open for a couple of years or, every once in a while, one will make it because they actually do one thing really well. You understand why they do it; it's like the restaurants now doing ghost kitchens. The thing is, many ghost kitchens look like their own brands. They just kind of dupe you into believing that. From personal experience, I know ghost brands don't deliver great food. It's as if the ghost brand is a side chick.

If you're going to try the ghost brand concept, my best suggestion is create two brands and put equal effort into them. In the same way a ghost kitchen uses an already existing kitchen, you could have two brands sharing the same kitchen. This has worked well for some companies over the years. One of those examples is the classic Pizza Hut / Taco Bell. You could order tacos or pizza through the same drive-through window or by walking in through the same front door using the same cash register.

But do you know why that worked? It worked because they didn't have a sign out front that said pizza, breadsticks, burritos, tacos, nachos, and frozen drinks. They had two distinct brands that told you exactly what they did. The brand names showed the separation between the two clearly.

We thought that was the coolest shit in the world. It didn't confuse us, nor did it seem complicated. We completely understood it was two separate restaurants operating out of the same building. We loved it because it was awesome to roll up and get a personal pan pizza, three crunchy tacos minus lettuce, and a Mountain Dew. So, if you're going to use a multi-brand strategy, whether it's two similar brands or two dissimilar brands, make sure you give them equal treatment.

In the case of the restaurants around here that show the Thai food, sushi, Korean BBQ, and Chinese food signs, it would be best if their owners picked just two. Then they can come up with two distinct brand names in which they would have two smaller signs instead of one large sign, for example. This would get them far more mileage than looking like they can do everything but nothing well. It's like that old saying about being an inch deep and a mile wide. Another saying talks about being a Jack of all trades and a master of none. What you can do is be really good at two separate things, especially if you can show the customer they're distinct.

The same thing happens with pizza joints that try to cross over and do a lot of subs and grinders. To me, you either do subs and grinders well or you do pizza well. But business owners often believe because they're so similar, that'll make sense to the public in the same way a Thai place can also make Korean BBQ.

You can try that under one name; it just makes sense to have two separate companies that look like they actually specialize in that particular product or service. What it comes down to is, the consumers aren't dumb and when you drive by and you look at that window, you have to think: what the hell is it they do there? They can make anything, but it is likely none of it will be good. Online ratings usually tell the rest of the story in this case.

This is not a new concept. It's just how human beings process information. If you're going to use a multi-brand strategy, go all in and build out each brand separately, even if they're under the same roof. Otherwise, the consumer will keep driving by your window, talking about trying your food one day, but they never will.

Kane's Conventional Take

Have you ever walked into a restaurant that serves Thai food, sushi, Korean BBQ, and Chinese cuisine? It's an odd mix, isn't it? You would think such a vast menu caters to everyone, but in reality, it often caters to no one.

This concept applies far beyond the culinary world, extending into various facets of business. Attempting to cater to all can actually result in appealing to none. Let's dive into why this strategy seldom works, backed by a real-world example.

Remember Yahoo? At its peak, Yahoo was a dominant player in the tech industry, but as time passed, its downfall became a cautionary tale for business owners everywhere. So what went wrong? Yahoo started as a simple, focused idea—a web directory to help users navigate the sprawling chaos of the early Internet. But over time, it morphed into a gargantuan creature, trying to be everything for everyone. It became a search engine, an email provider, a news portal, a shopping center, a social networking site, a photo-sharing platform, and more. It was like a restaurant serving Thai food, sushi, Korean BBQ, and Chinese food, except in the digital space.

Like our hypothetical multi-cuisine restaurant, Yahoo spread itself too thin, trying to cater to too many different tastes and losing its core identity in the process. Customers became confused about what Yahoo stood for, and that lack of a clear identity eroded their trust in the brand.

The ambition to cater to a broader audience isn't inherently wrong. Look, Google is an example of the strategy gone right. However, without a clear focus and understanding of your business's strengths and core values, the attempt to diversify can dilute the brand, confound the customers, and ultimately lead to an enterprise's downfall.

It's essential to know your business's strengths and stick to them. If your business is a sushi restaurant known for high-quality, fresh ingredients, don't try to sell Thai food, Korean BBQ, or Chinese food simply to cater to a wider demographic. You risk damaging the reputation you've built for exceptional sushi. Your regular customers may start to question whether your sushi is as fresh or as good now that your attention is split among four different cuisines.

This doesn't mean you should never diversify or expand your offerings. But when you do, it should be a calculated move that aligns with your business's identity, strengths, and values. It should be an expansion that amplifies what you're known for, not one that detracts from it.

Apple is an excellent example of this. It began as a computer company, and when Apple's leaders decided to diversify, they didn't venture into unrelated areas. Instead, they created products like the iPod, iPhone, and iPad that complemented and reinforced their reputation for designing sleek, user-friendly technology products.

When you try to be everything to everyone, like our Thai food, sushi, Korean BBQ, and Chinese food restaurant or Yahoo, you risk becoming a "jack of all trades, master of none." But when you focus on what you do best and stay true to your core, even while expanding, you become a master in your field. And the masters, as history has shown, tend to outlast and outperform the generalists.

So, as you contemplate your business's future, remember the restaurant that tried to serve every cuisine under the sun. Instead of seeking to cater to everyone, strive to serve a select group extraordinarily well. In the end, a focused, consistent offering will attract and retain more loyal customers than a scattergun approach ever will.

26

YOU CAN'T SELL WHAT'S NOT AVAILABLE

Kane's Measured Take

Imagine you're a passionate watch collector. You've saved up enough money, done your research, and decided to treat yourself with a Rolex Submariner, a timepiece you've dreamt about for years. You walk into a luxury watch boutique, your anticipation peaking. But your excitement quickly fades as the store manager apologetically informs you that the Rolex you want is out of stock. You might put your name on a waiting list or search another store, but how long would you wait before your patience wears thin and you consider buying a different, available brand? This scenario highlights a cardinal rule in business: you can't sell what's not available.

Even the most prominent companies can't ignore this fundamental principle. Luxury watch brands like Rolex, Patek Philippe, and Audemars Piguet suffer from the impact of this reality. Their tightly controlled distribution channels, coupled with limited production, often result in severe inventory shortages. While exclusivity can build desirability, when scarcity pushes potential customers to frustration and compels them to consider alternatives, it becomes a business problem.

Inventory management, especially for luxury items, can be a complex juggling act. Overstocking can lead to high carrying costs and markdowns if products don't sell as expected. On the other hand, understocking can result in lost sales and frustrated customers. Striking the right balance is crucial for ensuring customer satisfaction and profitability.

So how do companies deal with this challenge? One proven strategy is through floor plan financing. Essentially, floor plan financing is a revolving line of credit that allows a business to borrow against its inventory. Companies use this type of financing to purchase high-cost inventory that might not sell right away. Automotive dealerships and home appliance stores often use this method to keep their showrooms filled with a wide range of options.

In the context of luxury watch brands, floor plan financing can alleviate the inventory scarcity problem. By leveraging their high-value inventory, these companies can secure the funds needed to produce and stock more units. Retailers, in turn, can offer a broader selection of watches to potential buyers. Even if a particular model isn't available, the presence of alternative options within the same brand can deter a customer from defecting to a competitor.

That said, floor plan financing is not a silver bullet. It's a tool that, if used wisely, can help manage inventory challenges. But it can lead to overstocking and increased financial risk if used without a solid understanding of market demand. Therefore, companies should combine this strategy with reliable demand-forecasting methods to optimize their inventory levels.

Improving customer communication is another aspect that can mitigate the impact of inventory shortages. If a customer is after a Rolex Submariner and it's out of stock, instead of simply turning them away, the sales personnel can suggest placing an order for them, providing a realistic delivery timeframe, and keeping them updated on the order status. Such initiatives can turn a potentially negative customer experience into an opportunity for building stronger customer relationships.

Technology, too, plays an essential role in addressing this issue. With advancements in supply chain software, managers can have a real-time understanding of their inventory levels across various locations. They can make strategic decisions about stock allocation, ensuring products are available where they are most likely to be sold. Moreover, sophisticated data analytics can forecast demand more accurately, facilitating better inventory management.

The ability to sell a product is directly tied to its availability. It's a business reality that seems obvious, yet many companies overlook it. The luxury watch industry serves as a prime example where product scarcity can drive potential customers toward substitutes. By employing strategies like floor plan financing, improving customer communication, and leveraging technology, businesses can significantly enhance their inventory management, ensuring they always have something to sell. Because, after all, you can't sell what's not available.

James's Brazen Insight

We have a couple of stories for this topic. I am thinking back to a consulting project we were working on about fifteen years ago. It was a retail brand that was showing sales that were declining slowly, but declining nonetheless. Now it doesn't take a management consultant to figure this one out. The joint was so jam-packed with racks you could barely walk. So many clothes were packed on the racks you couldn't separate them to see the items.

It was a terrible shopping experience. We call this inventory creep. Slowly, over the years, like an overgrown apple tree, if you don't prune the inventory, it continues to stack and stack and stack. This is why we have sales a couple of times a year or a sidewalk sale: to offload this inventory. We want to offload this inventory for multiple reasons. First, we want to reclaim that capital so we can buy new inventory and turn that over. Second, we need to reclaim space as the store begins to get overcrowded. The third one is a combination of these: if we're going to take up space on a rack, why not take up space with something that sells? But let's not fill the space just with something that sells. Why not fill that space with something that sells over and over again?

The managers at big retail store conglomerates know how to manage their inventory properly. For sole proprietors or members of smaller regional groups with a handful of stores, inventory management may not be their strong point. It's one of those things that sometimes you have to sit down and show people the math. Each one of these slots is a revenue center, and this is why having items sitting there that don't sell is costing you money. Many business owners can't fathom having to lose money on inventory, regardless if they lose the money by a sale or by making a donation in order to get the items off the rack.

Let's think about it for a minute. If I have a rack with ten items on it that are not selling, and those items have a cost of $500 and we have to sell them on sale for $300, I just lost $200. But if that rack is full of items that sell four times a year instead of zero times a year, now I profit $200 for every time I turn that inventory. I'm now up $800. Yeah, I lost $200 liquidating old inventory, but now I can move things on which I actually make money.

Sometimes, we work with clients who have five to ten or fifteen stores. They're growing, but they're still thinking like a small business owner. When you do that, all that's ever going to get you is a small business.

We have another story that often goes along with small business thinking. This is the issue of not replenishing inventory because you're cashing that inventory in. You see this happen frequently where a business owner will run their inventory down because they want to take the cash out to pay personal bills or buy a new car or a new home instead of reinvesting that money in inventory. Now, if we think of every coat hanger or every square inch on the shelf as a revenue slot, but you're not filling those revenue slots with new inventory, how do you plan on continuing to make money? If you see inventory in a store is reduced by 50 percent, how can you be surprised when revenue drops by 50 percent?

It's our silly little saying: you can't sell something that's not there. Part of this is having the financial discipline to stay focused on the business. The other part of this is to not let your lifestyle get ahead of you, which traps many business owners. Most people get that. This is why, as entrepreneurs, we work so hard. We get no days off. We work around the clock or at least we're available around the clock. At some point, you want to reward yourself. But there is a time and a place to reward yourself and that's after all the business needs are taken care of.

Sometimes, you have to lose money on your inventory so you can get new inventory in and make money off of that. Other times, you have to increase inventory in order to deal with seasonal changes in demand and that might put a crimp on your personal lifestyle.

The goal here is to have your business perfectly merchandised with the right amount of inventory that people want to buy. At our base as humans, we are impulse buyers. And when someone has the urge to buy something, you want to make sure it is readily available for them to buy right now, before they talk themselves out of it. And this can't happen if it's not available because you ran the inventory down or you didn't offload old inventory to get the fresh new stuff in that everybody wants.

We live in a world where you can order anything online, but there are some days when you want it right now. Remind yourself of how you feel when you wake up in the morning and run down to the store to buy that thing and it isn't in stock. It's annoying. When it comes to servicing your customers, make sure when it's their time to buy today, you have it in stock and ready to go. Otherwise they'll spend that money somewhere else.

27

YOU'RE ONE HUNDRED PEOPLE EVEN WHEN YOU'RE FIVE

James's Fearless Approach

I've always been a big fan of hip hop as I grew up on it in the 1990s. In fact, I've even spent recent years producing a handful of hip hop and EDM albums for my music company. One interesting thing about hip hop and branding is that artists often portray themselves as more successful than they really are at that moment in time. This essentially helps bring a new audience in as they believe you're so successful that it's worth trying out your music.

Whether you have a bunch of custom jewelry or iced-out watches or the newest Bentley, there are several ways to show that you have all of that because of the success of your music. Technically, you can have all of this and never have dropped even a single song. This is no different than everyone else in the corporate world who has had to fake it until they made it.

See, there's no difference here from the dude who shows up to work wearing a new bespoke suit and a Rolex and pulls up in his certified pre-owned Porsche. Much of it is likely paid for on a credit card. This is not a new concept by any means. When you're unknown, people look for reasons to believe in you.

Going back to hip hop, I can think of a couple of the greatest moves people have made to posture up their net worth. One of those, from what I recall, is Birdman, who formed an oil company. I'm not sure anyone ever found out how much it made, but how many people can say they own a goddamn oil company? It's one of those things that is far greater than any car or home or piece of clothing you can buy. It's one of the greatest flexes you can have.

Another great example of doing something that puts you in that top tier is Jay-Z buying into the Brooklyn Nets. Some would say having ownership in or being an owner of a professional sports team is how we knight people in this country. Come to find out later, some sources said his stake in the NBA team was worth less than 1 percent and likely worth less than $500,000. But showing he was on such a higher level than anybody else in the rap game was more than worth it. How many artists own a chunk of a farggin' professional sports team?

If you own a startup or a small company trying to compete with much larger companies, you often have no choice but to make the same kind of moves that Birdman and Jay-Z did. I always say if you're one person, you need to look like ten. If your company has ten employees, it needs to look like it has one hundred. This is validated by how we live everyday life and judge people. The larger the company, the more successful it seems. If you look successful, there's a higher chance that whatever product or service you're delivering will also be worth it.

Another way this is proven is how valuations are done when you sell a company. If your company does less than $1,000,000 in revenue, it's actually very difficult to sell it. If it does $3–5 million, now it seems a little bit more stable and more people will be interested in it. Once you get to $10 million, now everybody wants a piece of you because there is stability in size. As you grow your company, remember people always see stability in size.

So how do you do this? How do you fake it until you make it? Well, we're not telling you to lie. But you need to do some things to make sure your company doesn't seem rinky-dink. Have a professionally built website with top-notch art. Make sure all your social media accounts have excellent photo selections and constantly produce new content.

You can technically open an office anywhere through places like WeWork. When you get the opportunity to make a great hire somewhere outside your local area, go for it. Now you're showing geographic diversity and you can show you have offices in other states, all while having access to a greater talent pool.

Everything from the photos on your website to how recently you posted on your website's blog comes into effect when someone is evaluating your business. If you're going into a sales presentation on Zoom, don't do it with just one person. Have three people on the call even if two of them are just sitting there quietly.

Think about all the experiences you had when working with larger businesses and mimic those. For example, one time we were on a phone call setting up a new Salesforce account for an internal CRM system. Even though it was for only a handful of users, Salesforce had four people on that sales call! Every touch point where a consumer will see, hear, or touch your brand needs to feel like it's much larger than it really is. We often say there's many things that shouldn't matter but do. And in this case, it's okay to be a boutique, but if you want to land more deals and make more sales, you also have to understand stability and size.

Kane's Structured Assessment

In the world of entrepreneurship and small businesses, perception can play a huge part in your success. One of the most enduring lessons I've learned is the power of embodying the entity you aspire to be, not the entity you currently are. In other words, even if you are a team of only five, act as if you are one hundred. This concept may seem counterintuitive at first, but let's dive into why this mindset is not just a motivational mantra, but a strategic imperative for growth and success.

First, adopting the mindset of a larger organization encourages growth. When you envision yourself as bigger, you naturally begin to plan and strategize at a scale that transcends your current state. This means you're more likely to take on larger projects, pitch to more prominent clients, and invest in capabilities you might not have considered otherwise. This state of being perpetually outside your comfort zone may feel uncomfortable at first, but it's an environment that fosters growth and innovation. By striving to meet the standards and expectations of a larger organization, you—and your team—are forced to adapt, evolve, and ultimately expand.

Second, this mindset impacts how your business is perceived externally. Clients tend to feel more comfortable dealing with larger, seemingly more established businesses. This is not a reflection of the quality of services small businesses provide, but rather a product of perceived stability, resources, and capacity larger businesses have. By projecting the image of a larger organization, you may be able to tap into opportunities that would otherwise be out of reach. It's about creating an impression of being bigger, better, and more capable, thus making you more attractive to prospective clients.

However, I must caution against dishonesty. This is not a call to deceive clients about your size or capabilities. Instead, it's about leveraging your strengths, amplifying your capabilities, and working smarter to project an image of professionalism and competency that rivals that of larger competitors. Be transparent, but highlight the advantages of your lean team, such as agility, personalized service, and dedicated attention.

Third, trust plays a pivotal role in business relationships. For many clients, dealing with a larger organization feels less risky. This perception stems from the assumption that larger businesses have a proven track record, established systems, and greater resilience to potential disruptions. As a small business owner, adopting the mindset and practices of a larger organization can help you build that trust. This means investing in professional communication tools, implementing robust processes, maintaining a professional online presence, and providing exceptional customer service.

Remember the goal is not to become a large, impersonal corporation but to combine the agility, passion, and personal touch of a small business with the professionalism, reliability, and scale of a larger one. It's about setting big, bold goals and pushing your boundaries while remaining true to your values and committed to your clients.

As a small business owner, you might have only five pairs of hands on deck, but that doesn't mean you can't make waves like a team of one hundred. Embrace the mindset of a larger organization and watch as you not only grow to meet the challenges but also redefine what's possible for your business. Always remember to act as if what you do makes a difference—because it probably does.

28

DECIPHERING CUSTOMER INSIGHTS & REVIEWS

James's Spirited Stand

Just this morning, I was thinking about online reviews from places like Amazon and Yelp. Later, I had a conversation with someone about restaurant reviews and how it seems like people are more inclined to complain than to leave a five-star review about how good the food was. But it also brings up the thought that, even if the business owner saw the bad review, would they listen? But we'll get to that in a moment.

Have you ever heard the line "I don't leave like that; I just leave?" It sums up how many people operate when it comes to leaving reviews, both good and bad. You're very unlikely to ever hear from a bulk of customers. Think about how many times you went to a restaurant and had a bad experience then went home without leaving a bad review. You just never went back. That "you only get one chance to make a first impression" rings true. Most of us when trying a new restaurant are likely to give it only one shot. In today's world, there's many other options that customers can try. The only time you get lucky is when the customer has been to your restaurant several times and they know you have good food, but they caught you on an off night.

When you realize how many insights businesses collect from their customers, it's pretty crazy. Those insights come from multiple sources, from feedback forms to online surveys to reviews online and nowadays reviews you send directly to the customer from your point of sale system. There's a lot of noise and you can't listen to every suggestion and complaint. The question becomes, can you see through the noise and see the patterns and the things you need to double down on or change?

Let's keep using restaurants as an example because we've all experienced this. You have a favorite restaurant that serves an amazing dish. Not just you but several other people love this dish. The next thing you know, it is pulled off the menu. Did you say anything or did you complain? Maybe you did and they didn't listen, or maybe you didn't at all. Perhaps not enough people complained for them to see that it was actually an issue. I feel like every time I find a restaurant that has something I really enjoy, somehow, two weeks later, they pull it off the menu. Just my luck, but that seems to be how it happens. The lesson here is pay attention to feedback from your customer base. All those little insights can keep you from making bad decisions and losing long-term customers.

Many companies now use their point of sale systems to collect reviews as a way to measure performance. The problem with this is, if your restaurant is positively reviewed, no one ever sees that because it's done in private. Now, that's a bonus if you're getting bad reviews and you don't want anyone to see them. It gives you time to fix it. On the other hand, if you own a four-star-plus restaurant and you're harvesting all these great reviews no one ever sees, what good is it? Sure it's good for measuring performance, but wouldn't it also be nice to have 2,000 reviews on Google with a 4.7 star rating?

It's already hard enough to get someone to give you one review anywhere. How many times have you checked out somewhere and the person at the cash register gave you a receipt, circled it, and told you to fill the survey out and you'd get a free gift card or a chance to win something. That's how hard it is to get a review these days. Can you imagine how hard it is to get two reviews from the same person?

If they're doing the review that's internal for your point of sale system, what are the chances they will go on Google or Yelp and leave you a second one? This isn't very likely unless it was a very negative review. We all know nothing motivates people more than a bad experience. People love to spread negativity.

Human behavior in the technological world is pretty nutty. We make decisions based on all the wrong data while at the same time thinking it's almost empirically correct. If we check an Amazon review and it has 3.8 stars, the likelihood of us ordering that product drops. But if you actually look at why the rating was so low and you find issues with the company shipping it but nothing wrong with the product, you would still order it. Well, that's if you dig a little deeper to find out for yourself. Many people just look at the rating number.

I'm sure Kane has data on this, but for every .1 of value on a Yelp review, you can increase or decrease a percentage of your sales. The difference between a 3.9 and a 4.2 can make a big difference in terms of how many customers come to your store.

We bring that up because in the same way as you're harvesting these customer insights, if your restaurant has only 200 reviews and your competitor half a mile down the road has 2,400, the new customer is more likely to visit the one with 2,400 reviews. So again, while you're internally collecting review data from your point of sale system, your online brand equity is suffering. You must balance harvesting customer insights and deciding what to do with them. Maintaining your outward image by playing silly psychological games in order to win is no longer an option.

It would be cool if we stopped looking at reviews and decided to try a place and said, "I'm going to try that today and find out for myself." But in this crazy world, we don't want to find out for ourselves anymore. We make decisions based on a bunch of people we never met, nor do we know their taste, but we take their reviews as gospel. As unfortunate as this is, at least you know the rules of the game. And now that you know the rules, you have to play to win.

Kane's Grounded Perspective

For businesses today, customer reviews aren't a sideline—they're the main event. Tapping into this powerful resource isn't about merely collecting ratings or testimonies; it's about decoding the sentiments and insights they offer.

Now, of course I have data to present (thanks, James!). Consider the restaurant industry. A 2011 Harvard Business School study discovered that a one-star increase in a restaurant's Yelp rating could boost its revenues by as much as 9 percent. That's no small potatoes. Think about it—this suggests that even a slight improvement in the public's perception can provide a solid bump to the top and bottom lines. But what does this mean for your business? The answer is simple: learning to interpret and utilize customer reviews can make the difference between merely surviving and truly thriving.

Let's begin with deciphering reviews. The simple numerical rating is an important piece of the puzzle, but it's far from the entire picture. Delve deeper into the written reviews, and you'll discover a wealth of insight. Customers often describe their experiences, voicing their satisfaction and dissatisfaction with specific aspects of your product or service.

What's the ambiance of your restaurant like? Is your e-commerce website user-friendly? Does your product deliver on its promises? It's not just about whether your customers had a good or bad experience. It's about why they had the experience they did.

Once you have a good understanding of what your customers are saying, the next step is to translate those insights into action. If several customers are praising your business's speedy delivery, that's a unique selling proposition you can capitalize on in your marketing efforts. On the other hand, if customers are repeatedly disappointed by a specific aspect of your product, it's a clear signal that there's room for improvement.

But it's not enough to just listen and react to customer feedback. The magic happens when you proactively engage with it. Responding to reviews—both positive and negative—can go a long way in showcasing your commitment to customer satisfaction. A *Harvard Business Review* study found that responding to customer reviews results in better ratings.

In the face of a negative review, the instinct might be to ignore it or get defensive. But this is an opportunity to turn a negative into a positive. A thoughtful, professional response that acknowledges the issue and outlines the steps taken to rectify it can improve the perception of your business. Additionally, featuring your positive reviews in your marketing material can boost your reputation. Testimonials serve as social proof, convincing potential customers your product or service is worth their time and money.

Reviews are not just a digital-age version of word of mouth; they are powerful tools that can provide deep customer insights and significantly influence your company's reputation and revenues. Decoding and acting on these reviews are steps that businesses—big or small—can't afford to ignore.

Remember customers who take the time to write a review are giving you something valuable: their perspective. Their voice is a gift that can guide your business toward better products, improved customer service, and, ultimately, a stronger bottom line. Treat it with the respect it deserves. It's time to dive into the gold mine of customer insights and reviews, decipher the messages, and let them illuminate your path to success.

29

NEVER GIVE YOUR CUSTOMERS A REASON TO TRY SOMETHING ELSE

James's Fiery Assessment

Over time, if you read enough of my stuff, you'll realize I'm a foodie at heart. I use a lot of restaurant examples as I dine out often, have invested in hospitality ventures, and even have a few of my own concepts coming to life. So in the case of this chapter, I'm going to use another restaurant reference.

There was a time when I would eat at this Mexican food chain three or four or more times a week. You'll read about this often from me as it was a business lesson I really took to heart. As much as I hate to admit it, I sometimes ate it twice a day. I'd eat it so much I would go to two different locations like I was a crack addict so the employees didn't see my face so frequently. Technically, with all of the sodium I ate, crack may have been healthier. I loved the chicken and queso so much, I was addicted.

Then came issues with the food. People were getting sick, so I stopped going, or going as much anyway. Obviously, not everyone stopped, but the incidents did slow sales down quite a bit. But you wouldn't know that today by looking at their stock price as it went absolutely to the moon. Here's why it took so long to get those customers back. People form habits and they get into grooves. You sink into those grooves so deeply you can only see in front of you.

I was in the groove of eating there almost every day for lunch and then that habit was broken. Now that my habit was broken, I had to find somewhere else to eat. Then I realized how many new places had opened, which allowed me to find a couple of new favorites. This also had me going to places like Qdoba. The queso just hits differently when it's in the burrito, straight tasty AF. Not only did I have a reason to find something new, the situation encouraged me to try the competition. Had that issue never arisen, I probably would have stayed in my habit for much longer. Instead, I was about ready to bathe myself in Qdoba queso.

Post COVID, I've had other issues with the first restaurant in this scenario, to the point where I basically don't eat there anymore and, if I do, it's very rarely. To be honest, there's so many damn choices now that if I have to spend fifteen bucks on lunch, I'm not going to settle.

Another example of not giving your customers a reason to try the competition comes from a consulting project we were working on last year. This project involved a rapidly expanding franchise in the QSR space with a tremendous amount of competition. It had a superior product and continues to have one to this day. Nonetheless, with increasing food cost and labor, inflation has pinched everybody. The client wanted to eliminate some specials and happy hour like many bars and restaurants often have from 2:00 p.m. to 5:00 p.m. or 3:00 p.m. to 6:00 p.m., for example. For our customers, we had to present the question: would you rather break even on happy hour or make a small profit versus give your customers a reason to try your competitor?

It's a tough question to answer. We typically come from the mindset that once you get your hooks into a customer, you don't ever let go. We know from years of consulting and growing businesses that it probably costs twice as much to get an old customer back than it did to acquire them in the first place. According to the math, you're likely better off just breaking even on the happy hour sales, knowing they're going to continue to be your customer and come back on Saturday, when you can make a nice profit.

A lot of times as business owners and entrepreneurs, we believe our product is so good no one would ever go anywhere else. But, as a foodie, I must tell you, somehow you always end up finding that next place you love. The last thing I want is one of my loyal customers to try my competitor's food and find out they have some recipe they love. Never give someone the opportunity or a reason to try something else.

It also feels like in the past decade or so, customers have become more fickle. Loyal customers still exist, especially those that are fans of your brand regardless of whether it's food, retail brands, or even a sports team. But how much they're willing to tolerate and stay loyal is wavering. We've learned as the world has changed that when you have endless options, you realize you don't have to put up with as much as you used to. Maybe as humans we used to be more understanding, but certainly in a post-COVID world we are not.

If you had a bad experience at a hotel or a restaurant, you thought maybe you just caught them on a bad night. Now, if your breadbasket doesn't come out in the first five minutes, you jump on Yelp and start writing a bad review.

We can also give a couple instances of where poor service has resulted in the opportunity for the customer to try somewhere new that resulted in a poor outcome as well. My kids are at the age where they got into golf last summer, so I found a local PGA pro to coach them.

Things went very well for a couple of months. Unfortunately, one day when we arrived to get our cart, the person who runs that cart operation was extremely rude. He essentially told us that since we weren't playing golf, we weren't allowed to have a cart and that two little kids carrying their bags and I should walk to the back of the practice range, which was probably about three-eighths of a mile. With lessons, you get the cart; it's all part of the fee.

I don't roll like that and disrespecting me isn't going to get you very far. At some point in the past, it may have ended up getting you something else. Okay, that's neither here nor there. Like for most people, common courtesy and respect is high amongst my priorities. It wasn't just the fact that he said that. He was really rude about it. I've never had anyone talk to me like that, not even at 7-Eleven at 2:00 a.m. on a Friday. Funnily enough, when I read the online reviews, I found multiple complaints about this individual from golf club members. I saw a pattern of a company that knows they have a problem but don't want to deal with it. The ridiculous part is, this was a customer-facing person who was causing the club great damage. I told the PGA pro we'd do the scheduled lesson, but I might look around. Like we said before, never give your customers a reason to look somewhere else. It wasn't the pro's fault, but the club made money on the lessons and green fees, so he too lost.

I came across a better coach who was closer to home who had his own indoor studio with four golf simulators. This gentleman also runs a division two school program and has many valuable leads in the golf world. It benefited me to look around, but it didn't benefit the PGA pro because he lost a customer who was paying full freight for two kids to get private lessons.

Here's a similar story to go with that. It does seem like customer service is out the window in this world. But, if you choose to focus on that, it's highly likely you will stomp the hell out of all your competitors. Focus on customer service and it's unlikely you'll lose.

The gym I've been going to for a very long time started to suffer from a lot of customer service issues. Also, I was using one of their personal trainers, who I enjoyed working with very much. It sounded like the management there wasn't the greatest, and my personal trainer had a falling out with the management team. Employees come and go, so I can't say that alone made me look somewhere else. If you add everything up they did, it incentivized me to look around at other gyms, though.

I ended up choosing another gym located about ten minutes further away. I found a new trainer who I now see four or five days a week. I also enjoy working out at this gym. I never would have thought to look at this place if my experience at the old gym had been at least decent. Spending a tremendous amount of time evaluating gyms is not high on my priority list. I like to lift a heavy weight, put it back down again, and do it again.

This isn't rocket science, and I can do that almost anywhere. It's not like shopping for car insurance and trying to save $4,000 a year.

If my old gym hadn't pushed me to look somewhere else, I probably would have stayed there another ten years. I would have tried out a couple of trainers there and found someone to replace the gentleman I used to work out with. They just made too many mistakes and they allowed me to look somewhere else.

The grass isn't always greener. People often find that out in relationships or when they choose to leave their employer. In business, we say everyone's replaceable until they're not. I wrote something similar in my other books, *Headwind* and *Second Act*. When it comes to relationships, sure there's 8 billion people in this world, so it's rather likely you'll find someone equal or better if you look long enough. But that doesn't mean you don't want the person who's gone. When it comes to products and services, you more than likely will always be able to find something better and you'll quickly forget about your old favorite.

That doesn't mean you want to take the time, energy, or effort to do it. It's fun trying new restaurants, but those experiences can be bad as well. If you try enough, you'll eventually find a new place you love that you wouldn't have normally tried if your original favorite restaurant hadn't pushed you to try it. The easy takeaway on this one is that once you have a customer who is loyal and has a habit of using your service or product, never give them a reason to try something else, as we have said once, twice, and maybe three times now. It's expensive to get new customers, but it's really expensive to get old customers back.

Kane's Practical Analysis

At the core of any successful business are satisfied, loyal customers. In the world of digital marketing, this translates into two vital metrics—customer acquisition cost (CAC) and lifetime value (LTV). While CAC measures the resources you expend to acquire a new customer, LTV indicates the net profit attributed to the entire relationship with a customer. Optimizing these metrics is pivotal, and one surefire way of doing so is simple yet profound: never give your customers a reason to try someone else.

For starters, let's examine why keeping a customer is so valuable. Numerous studies have looked at the effect of a small percentage of improvement in customer retention and its profound impact on profitability. The logic is intuitive—returning customers buy more and are cheaper to market to given the trust already established.

So how do we prevent customers from seeking alternatives? First, the most apparent reason a customer might look elsewhere is dissatisfaction with your product or service. Whether it's a smartphone that crashes frequently or a coffee shop where the lattes are lukewarm, quality issues are a direct invitation for customers to try your competitors. Prioritizing quality isn't just a tactic. It's a philosophy that must permeate every layer of your organization.

Second, your product might be stellar, but if your customer service is lacking, you're giving customers a reason to look elsewhere. According to a study by American Express, more than half of Americans have scrapped a planned purchase or transaction due to bad service. Ensure your customer service is responsive, empathetic, and capable of solving problems quickly and effectively.

Third, consistency breeds trust. Customers return because they know what to expect. If you're inconsistent, customers may choose a competitor they perceive as more reliable. This applies to all aspects of your business—product quality, customer service, branding, and communication.

Fourth, engaged customers are loyal customers. Keep your customers engaged with regular, relevant, and personalized communication. Whether it's a monthly newsletter, a personalized discount offer, or a simple thank-you note, every interaction is an opportunity to reinforce your relationship with your customer.

Finally, just because your customers love your product today doesn't mean they won't jump ship when something newer and better comes along. Staying ahead of the curve requires constant innovation. Regularly update your products, anticipate your customers' changing needs, and always look for ways to improve.

Apple is a great example of a company that does customer retention well. Its products, although priced higher than those of most competitors, are renowned for their quality and consistency. Apple's customer service, both online and at physical Apple Stores, is a key part of the brand. Through regular product updates and improvements, those who work at Apple manage to keep their customer base engaged and resistant to switching, despite attractive alternatives.

However, no discussion on retaining customers would be complete without mentioning the role of value. Customers need to perceive that the value they derive from your product or service outweighs the cost. If the balance shifts and the cost—financial, time, or effort—outweighs the value, they'll start exploring alternatives. Regularly assess your value proposition and adjust as necessary in order to ensure it aligns with your customers' perceptions and expectations.

Keeping a customer involves a holistic approach that includes excellent product quality, superb customer service, consistency, engagement, innovation, and compelling value. By ensuring these elements, you minimize the risk of giving your customers a reason to try someone else, thereby optimizing your CAC and LTV, and, most important, fostering a loyal and engaged customer base.

SECTION
THREE
GROWTH

30

JUST BECAUSE YOU BUILD IT, DOESN'T MEAN THEY WILL COME

James's Aggressive Thoughts

How many times have you seen a new place open and you knew it wasn't going to make it? This just happened down the street from my HQ. Someone decided to open a "fancy" hot dog joint in the middle of a business district with endless lunch options within a one-mile radius. Sure, Portillo's kills it in downtown Chicago, but this wasn't Portillo's, nor are we in Chicago anymore, Toto.

There wasn't a lack of hot dogs in the area, and people in general didn't want to spend seven to nine dollars for one. You can put black truffles and 24k gold flakes on it, but people still won't spend that much on a hot dog in this market. It's metro Detroit. We eat cheap Coneys then sit around and argue about which restaurant has the best one.

At this new place, the food was okay, the branding was questionable, and the location was wrong. And that's before we even talk about how high the triple-net lease was on that Class A retail spot. Do you know how many hot dogs you must sell to cover that lease? Maybe they had fat margins, but I don't want to pimp hot dogs all day to grind out a few bucks a year.

Every day, the next big startup is creating a solution for a problem that doesn't exist. After they blow through millions to find that out, they pivot. Then they pivot again and again. It's like making four right turns in a row just to end up back on the same damn road again. Why do that when you could just open Waze? Waze wanted me to drive through the brick wall of a liquor store because it thought a road was there, but that is a conversation for another time.

With that story, you now know not to bring something to the market the consumer wasn't asking for. While Steve Jobs may have thought you have to tell the consumer what they want, this isn't the case for most businesses. You must do your research. Conduct polls and surveys, get boots on the ground and talk to people, sit in front of places and look at what the average customer looks like, and more. Keep digging for insights until you get the yes or no answer that the market wants and or needs what I am selling.

You can love a product or service personally, but the masses may not want it. It could be a great product or service in this state, but in another state, it may not be as demographics and demand change. Ever notice that the wealthier areas have fewer fast-food restaurants? Yet where I grew up in a working-class area, we had all of them. Understand your core customer and what makes them tick. Make sure you're solving a problem or appealing to someone's needs or desires. Otherwise, you'll be the hot dog joint that no one wanted to eat at.

Kane's Realistic Understanding

The world is full of great ideas that never came to fruition. Great ideas that don't see the light of day because of the inventor's laziness are criminal. Great ideas that don't materialize because of a lack of product-market fit are a shame. Great ideas, however, that are a good idea and have proven their ability to find a home with customers, but haven't yet crossed the chasm from early adopters to mass market consumption, are a marketer's dream. Today's marketer has an abundance of tools at their fingertips to match products with the right customers: search engine optimization, paid ads, social media, email marketing, podcasts, blog content, and the list goes on and on.

A great quote often floats around the Internet: "If you have a business but don't take marketing seriously, you have a hobby." The mistake rookie entrepreneurs and marketers make when bringing a product to market is focusing so hard on the product itself that it takes away from the requisite attention on making sure the market knows your product exists. Yes, spend money, time, and resources on a beautiful website and packaging for your innovative Bluetooth earbuds that charge by the sun. But make sure to spend just as much money, time, and resources (if not more) on your go-to-market strategy and marketing plan. The world is full of solar-powered Bluetooth earbuds. Innovations like that are a dime a dozen. Where products achieve a real competitive advantage is in marketing execution. Look, just because you build it, doesn't mean they will come.

Remember Google Plus? What about Google Glass? These are two canonical examples of products that seemed innovative, deserved to be brought to market, but failed miserably because of a lack of marketing focus. Google Plus was billed as a direct competitor to Facebook in the days when there was still significant market share to compete for in the nascent social media scene. But where Facebook had a clear target demographic—younger, college-aged individuals sharing their lives with their circle of friends—an attempt at customer analysis for Google Plus typically comes up short. With good products, it's never a challenge to quickly identify a target market. Who was Google Plus built for? What was its main purpose? Surely it was more than a glorified password manager.

The same goes for Google Glass. Back in 2015, I attended a Google Glass event in Detroit, just when Google was rolling out publicity for the product. Needless to say, I left the event more confused about the applications of Google Glass than I was going into the event hall. That's not good. A visual aid that hooks up to the Internet seemed like a neat idea at the time, but without proper marketing execution (identifying target customers, understanding the competitive landscape, optimizing the product's capabilities), all we were left with as eager Google Glass enthusiasts were dashed hopes about an exciting innovation that never was. All because the Mountain View behemoth thought that just because you build it, they will come.

31

MARKETING IS EXPENSIVE: ONE DOLLAR OUT TO GET SEVENTY CENTS IN

Kane's Sensible Approach

As a marketer, you give yourself a promotion from theorist to true practitioner the day you choose to run ads for your product or service. It's daunting to put money on the line with the expectation that you need to generate some level of return on investment. Running ads for your business is a lot like taking the leap from recreational golfer (Is this a gimme?) to counting each and every stroke in a tournament environment (Will I be able to make contact with the golf ball when my arms are trembling like this?).

I've run paid ad campaigns for many different clients providing all sorts of products and services. You name it, I've probably run a paid ad for a similar product or service. The main lesson to take on board when engaging in paid marketing? It's. Damn. Expensive. And it's getting more and more expensive every day. As advertising on Google, Facebook, and other platforms becomes a tax businesses must absorb or risk relegation to obscurity, the field gets more saturated and auction bids inevitably go up.

If you spend any time on social media, you've probably been served an ad pitching you some drop shipping course where you can make a fortune running ads for toilet paper that gets shipped direct to customers—at great margins to you. These courses are bullshit. Trust me, I've tried. Just like the stock market, if there really was an arbitrage opportunity with paid ads, it's probably been starched away by the time you get around to running your ad campaigns.

That said, there is a way to win with paid ads—understanding customer lifetime value (CLV) and playing the long game. Unless you're selling a high-efficacy pharmaceutical cure, most businesses should be looking to attract customers who make repeat purchases or buy multiple products and services. A customer viewed through the lens of the total number of purchases they make with your company is far more valuable than just the initial transaction. This informs CLV and is crucial to making paid ads work for you.

Napkin math time. Let's say you sell a $100 widget, but your typical customer buys one widget a year for fifteen years. You have a CLV of approximately $1,500. Now, instead of trying to make paid ads work on unit economics of $100, you have the more realistic target of acquiring a customer for anything less than $1,500 minus operating expenses. The key to making paid ads work for you is to reframe your goal. Instead of thinking you need to be profitable with every click or impression your paid ad motivates, paid ads should be used to acquire customers who have a favorable CLV for your business. Not every customer you can identify is a profitable customer. Use paid ads to target high CLV customers only—do your three C's analyses to figure out who these customers are.

One more note. Unfortunately, the cost of running ads isn't the only expense marketing practitioners need to pay attention to. For a client looking to supercharge lead generation, we once built a paid ad campaign that was so successful (through paid ads, we generated ~300 percent more leads each day) it overwhelmed the client's sales team. When you're confident in your ability to formulate paid ad campaigns that will succeed, then you need to shift the client's attention to sales infrastructure. Do you have the sales team and capabilities in place to process and close the results of a wildly successful paid ad campaign? If not, just stop. Focus on building a sales process that can support your marketing efforts. Otherwise, you're just setting good money on fire. Don't do that.

James's Unrestrained Perspective

Right now, someone is cussing out Google AdWords because they spent $500 on ads last week and brought in only $200 in sales. This happens to anyone who has developed or run any kind of ads on the radio, TV, digital and beyond. We all love that dream of spending one dollar on marketing to bring in five. We want to believe it can't be that hard to scale! Scale! Scale! It is just like every article you read about some new hot tech entrepreneur who seems to know only the words *scale* and *pivot*, except scaling isn't easy and it's tougher on the pocketbook than most are ready for.

Acquiring leads and especially new customers is really pricey. To top it off like you do a chocolate sundae at a Vegas buffet, we also live in a world where instant gratification is expected. Frustration sets in when we don't get it and we throw tantrums like a two-year-old with an empty Pez dispenser because "none of this business stuff is ever easy." If it was easy, everyone would do it and become rich.

The general rule of ad spend is that awareness campaigns rarely return your money dollar for dollar within a short window of time. You must look at your lifetime customer value then run the math to figure it out. Let's use an example of a group of restaurants I'm invested in. If I spend $500 on ads to bring in thirty customers and $350 in sales, you can't look at it and say, "Oh, you lost $150."

What it comes down to is I was able to acquire new customers for about $16 each. Of the thirty customers, if fifteen come back one more time, we bring in another $175. Even if just five of the original thirty become long-time customers, visiting our restaurants five times a year for three years, we are way up on that marketing spend now. Figuring out and tracking your lifetime customer value is something every marketer must do if they ever want to fully understand the ROI of their campaigns.

This is why you can't sit around and plan to scale quickly just through an increased ad spend. It's a slow build, and over time more and more people become aware of your brand. As you gain loyal customers, you have the word-of-mouth effect. So you may spend $500 to acquire thirty new customers, which is $16 each roughly, but those thirty customers tell their friends and bring you six new customers. Now the reality is you're acquiring customers for about $13.80 each, which means it takes even less time to recoup your investment. Marketing for scale isn't magic; it's science. Keep in mind that it's a marathon and not a sprint. So, carb load on some pasta, get a good night's rest, and understand it will all pay off one day, just not today.

32

YOUR NEXT BIG UNLOCK? UNDERSTAND YOUR CUSTOMER (DEEPER)

James's Tenacious Take

Assuming makes an … out of me … and an … out of you. You get my point. You can't assume who your customer is and what they want. It's going to take a much deeper understanding. If it was that easy, there would be a music recommendation app that could actually predict what I want to listen to next. Except right now I am playing DMX and the next track is Linkin Park, then Tori Amos, and after that Hans Zimmer Live in Prague, so good luck with figuring that out. You would have to pick my brain to fully understand what makes me tick across that music selection. Give me an electric violin, a ninety-three-key Bösendorfer, and some heavy bass from 808s. We can talk about those another time; it's hard to explain.

This is what Clayton Christensen once spoke about during his tenure at Harvard. He gave a speech on why customers were buying milkshakes for breakfast. You could take a million guesses why, but they had to dig to understand why, which is the key to scaling (that word again). This is what we live for—to understand the "why" so we can do more of it.

To many, marketing is throwing darts at a wall while hoping you hit a bull's-eye. When you do this without any insights, it's the equivalent of playing darts blindfolded after drinking four double Jamesons (well, Jameson does make for a hell of a night anyway). Even worse, you end up burning through money like the government during COVID, leaving you wondering where it all went.

Understanding the why takes an open mind. You have to constantly observe customer behaviors and patterns along with trying to make sense of things that don't make sense, such as who the hell buys a milkshake for breakfast? Well, now we know why, well *we* do, so I won't spoil it for you—go look up the video on YouTube. You'll enjoy it.

One other thing to think about after watching that milkshake lecture as it was many years ago. If you think about it in today's terms, how many people roll through a Starbucks every morning and order a dessert like Frappuccino, FOR BREAKFAST? So we couldn't wrap our minds around a milkshake for breakfast, but a Frappuccino hits just right. It's just a matter of how you approach the insight.

I'll use another restaurant example. One of the restaurants we own is in a business district that has a lot of industrial buildings. Sales are often slow during the week at the time of opening. I had to put myself in the mindset of those workers, who often work from 6:00 a.m. to 2:00–3:00 p.m. During my technology consulting years, I often worked in plants like this. I would get there at 6:00–7:00 a.m., so by 10:30 a.m., I was already thinking about lunch. It was a much different schedule than working in Chicago, where you get to the office a little later and eat lunch at noon or 1:00 p.m. If you're a true Wall Streeter, you know lunch is for wimps.

The lesson here was, we started opening earlier, then received a flood of orders right before 11:00 a.m. so customers could pick up their lunch by 11:15. Some big chains start serving lunch at 10:30 a.m. for a reason, and it's because they understood the "why."

Kane's Measured View

Arguably the most useful, innovative, and influential product of the past decade has been Amazon Prime. We get so much utility for fifteen dollars a month: free two-day shipping, access to an enormous catalog of products, discounts at Whole Foods Market, and the list goes on and on. If you've ever wondered how Amazon Prime remains viable at such a low relative cost, the answer is that the company banks on some users being heavy users and some users not using it as much—essentially spreading the cost of the service across a large number of customers and tapping into the power of numbers. It's a lot like how insurance companies spread risk (and cost) across a large customer base. For heavy users of Amazon Prime, the consumer surplus generated on a membership must be enormous. So, while Amazon Prime can boast a membership of around 150 million users, why isn't everyone who lives in a country with access to Prime a member of the service?

The answer lies in an important lesson many marketers learn too late: not everybody is an ideal customer for your product or service. Very few products or services have universal utility, and even if you argue that your product or service does, it's most likely that not every customer would be profitable. Understanding who your ideal customers are is a huge unlock for a business, and the ability to generate customer insights is what separates rookie marketers from those who can truly effectuate results.

The reason is tied back to an understanding of CLV, the Pareto principle, and the idea that businesses should commit to servicing the most profitable customers first. I pose this question to you: if you had ten individuals standing in front of your store, each with different levels of profitability to you, and you could service only four, which four would you let into your store? You'd choose the four most profitable customers first. And while business in real life is a lot more convoluted because all businesses are resource-constrained at some level (you only have so much capacity to service so many clients), the same equation is at play. The beauty of being a marketer in today's data-driven age is that we can determine which of those four customers to let into our store. Rookie marketers guess. Skilled practitioners, however, seek out the data and information to understand the characteristics and traits of customers who, in the long run, skew toward the more profitable archetype.

It can seem unnatural or counterintuitive to look at the playing field and decide certain customers are worth more than others to your business. But the reality is that not every dollar is the same—some dollars are more easily generated than others. If, as a marketer, you can provide your organization with leads that not only give you the best chance of great profitability but also cause the least amount of strain on your organization's resources, it is in your and your organization's best interest to do whatever it takes to find these leads (and customers).

33

THE KEY TO MAKING ADVERTISING WORK? CAPTURE THE LEAD

Kane's Commonsense View

The best marketing feels like a one-on-one conversation between the consumer and the brand. This is why much of the talk about marketing innovation over the past few years has been about personalization: how can brands better understand the traits, preferences, and buying patterns of each and every customer and then meet those customers where they are? Technology allows marketers to tap into more granular levels of insight than ever before. Think about your own buying habits. Don't you love it when brands serve you exactly what you want, when you want it, and how you want it?

If you've ever run ads for your company, you already know how tricky it is to generate and maintain decent levels of ROI. It's such a wasted opportunity to do the hard work of attracting a potential consumer to your website or store and then let them leave without knowing they were there, who they are, and what they were searching for. But this is a mistake I've seen—and been guilty of—countless times. Marketers will spend vast sums of resources and time perfecting the language on an ad, beautifying the word structure, using terms that attract only the target audience and repelling those who are not the intended audience, but then bang their heads against their desk as more and more dollars are spent on ad clicks that generate no orders. It's a vicious and frustrating cycle.

The rookie mistake marketers make is not being completely ruthless about capturing the lead. It doesn't matter if you have to deploy pop-ups on your website every twenty-five seconds, throw sign-up forms on every landing page, or put content behind walls. Do whatever it takes to make sure as many people as possible who land on your website (or come into your store) leave contact information. Hell, even if it's JUST an email address or a phone number, that is better than nothing. Why is this so important? It goes back to the principle that great marketing is a conversation—and the only way to have a conversation with someone is to have a way to reach them first.

Think of the last purchase you made that was triggered by direct marketing tactics—so a brand emailed or texted you and that resulted in a purchase. I'm a big fan of Crown and Caliber, the timepiece marketplace, and they send me a text message nearly every day at lunchtime. Most days, it's a one-sided conversation. But on some days, when I have a free moment, the conversation is reciprocated—I click on the link they send me and look around the website. This conversation is possible only because they captured my information at some point in the past—just a phone number. Be ruthless about capturing information from prospective customers. Whether you're running advertising spend or relying solely on organic means of generating traffic to your company assets, think of every interaction as an opportunity to start a conversation with a future customer.

James's Steadfast Perspective

Every marketer wants to show up to the all-hands-on-deck sales meeting with the good leads. Not just the good leads, the Glenngary leads. We know only the great salespeople get the good leads, and coffee is for closers. Now, maybe your sales and marketing meeting isn't as intense as Alec Baldwin in that movie, but if you cannot capture great leads for your sales team, how do you plan on them making any sales?

But it's tough. How do you capture leads without becoming annoying? How many damn contact forms do I need to add to this site before someone actually fills it out? Then you read Hotjar stories of watching browsing behavior and people just fly by all of your forms and contact pages with reckless abandon. If you don't know about Hotjar, check it out. We aren't sponsored by Hotjar, but their videos are a cool way to understand consumer web behavior.

Let's continue on this journey of harvesting leads without being annoying. For example, we have all resisted doing a pop-up on our websites. We lived in fear that it would turn our brand into a place that feels like spam central, kind of like that episode of *The Chappelle Show* where Dave walked through a mall that was reimagined as the Internet in real life, where he had every kind of ad and spam coming at him from all directions. It's an old-school episode that was funny yet true at the same time.

But guess what? The last website we worked on added a pop-up to increased leads by over 50 percent. Not only did it increase leads, but it also significantly boosted the ROI on running Google AdWords. Whereas that site used to spend a lot on ads to get a few conversions but a lot of bounce traffic, they started to capture those leads with an exit intent pop-up before they bounced. This allowed our customer to increase ROI from the ads while lowering the cost to acquire a new customer. And when we find something that works, what do we do? We scale it! See the trend here? Find what doesn't work and stop doing it. Find what works and do more of it.

Now you're thinking, "Oh, no; I don't want to do a pop-up!" Well, maybe you shouldn't. One size doesn't fit all when it comes to capturing leads. Maybe you need to redesign your contact forms or get an email field in the hero area to sign up for a newsletter or discount. Maybe you need to do a downloadable asset that is of value, it can't just be anything otherwise people won't go through the trouble. Do a research report with a survey, for example. This will take some work, but if you want results, you have to do the tough things others aren't willing to do.

Don't be afraid of header plugins, pop-ups, cart abandonment emails, and everything in between. There is only one thing you can do. Test, test, and test until you figure out what works the best to capture leads and then run with it. The quick insight is, it's okay to piss a few people off as collecting some leads is better than collecting none.

34

GO WHERE THE AIR IS THINNER

James's Forceful Approach

Be the highest in the room, and I'm not talking about Travis Scott, although that is one hell of a track. It's also the loudest in the room with a mix and master by Mike Dean.

The concept of going where the air is thinner is that there is simply less oxygen for the less capable to survive. Certain vultures can fly as high as 37,000 feet. How many natural predators do they have to face at that height? None, unless it's a 757 on its way up to FL390. If you haven't noticed, we are a world in a constant race to the bottom. We often find excuses and justifications to do the easy things even if they won't yield us the results we need.

What do we do? We compete on the cheaper price. Have you ever noticed how much more competition there is at the bottom than the top? Sure, it's lonely at the top, but it's the top! It's fine if you want to school yard scrap in the gutter with everyone else doing the easy things, but keep in mind you're going to get exactly what they get, which often isn't much.

Let's use the example of TV commercials. To shoot a great video takes budget, a creative eye, a good producer \ director \ script plus post editing, and if you want to do it right, you also need a top-notch colorist. We have done great videos for companies like Employment BOOST that all said and done was probably around $10,000, but that could have easily been $50,000. Even if you have the budget, it doesn't mean you can buy the right creative. Nailing the creative part is hard.

So what's cheaper and easier than this? Logging on to Google, typing in a bunch of headlines for your AdWords, and running ads all day on search results. And while you're doing that, everyone else is packed in a room full of your competitors, who keep upping the bid on the ads, making your ROI go down faster than Pershing Square Capital's investment in Netflix.

This is the lesson: if it's easy to do, everyone will do it and ruin it. Yes, that kind of rhymes and it's not intentional, but I kind of like the ring to it. Do the hard things you know others won't. It's not that hard to outwork people these days. Brute force rarely fails when you're doing a lot of the right work. Focus on the ultra-creative and do things at the highest level. Never settle. Writing blog posts is a low-yield way of getting PR pickups, but it's cheap and easy. Hell, even dogs have blogs now. What's harder? Commissioning a survey and writing up a five-page publication with a synopsis, charts, and all that fun visually pleasing stuff. Now, send that off to reporters and see how many pickups you get. It's less crowded at the top for a reason, and the more time you spend doing the hard things others can't or aren't willing to do, the better your chances of winning.

Kane's Careful Consideration

The reason marketing is challenging is because the airwaves are completely saturated with sales messaging. Thousands of products and services promise to fix every conceivable ailment or need, and we, as consumers, are bombarded with marketing all day long. When we're catching up on the news, we're sure to see an ad. When we're busy navigating airports to get from one destination to the next, we're sure to take in an ad or three. When we're mindlessly scrolling social media, we're certain to be served an ad for sustainable cotton sneakers—whether you need new shoes or not. With all this noise, figuring out how to get your brand or company to stand out from the crowd is nearly impossible. But that's where the opportunity lies.

When marketers or business operators think about solving the visibility problem for their company or brand, the first idea is usually running an ad on social media or grabbing stock video content and putting together a crappy spot on cheap, streaming television. The best marketers, however, go where the air is thinner. They do the harder work. They design something creative, lean on informative data, and aren't afraid to invest real money to bet on their own ideas and strategies.

It's one thing to get your local newspaper to write a quick glam piece on your company's launch or new product. It's another thing to commission a survey, gather real data from real people out in the world, and come up with an informative perspective on a relevant, hot-button issue—and go to the press with a strategy to gain mass market media coverage.

Instead of taking an amateur photograph of your new product and running minimal advertising, hoping for the best, go where the air is thinner. What is the harder, more rewarding avenue you can take as a marketer that will truly separate what you are doing from what every other marketer out there is doing? Is it spending a little bit more money to come up with a beautiful thirty-second television spot you can run on national news channels? Is it hiring a professional voiceover artist to craft an informative, entertaining twenty-second clip you can run on the radio in your target markets? Is it starting a YouTube channel or podcast where you host on-brand conversations with leaders in your industry—gaining recognition as an individual (or brand) with a real perspective and something to say?

You should be able to see what I'm getting at—by going where the air is thinner, you're doing the things other marketers won't do, precisely because they are more difficult, more challenging, and ultimately more rewarding and newsworthy because they are actually interesting. The world has enough stories of boring store launches and press releases of manufactured collaborations between brands that have no business working together. Be the brand with something interesting to say. Go and do cool shit. Be creative. I guarantee you it's worth it.

35

PROTECT YOUR BRAND AT ALL TIMES

James's Candid Thoughts

When you're born into this world, the doctor usually smacks you on the ass to see if you cry. What they should do right after that is say, like they do in boxing, keep your hands up and protect yourself at all times! The cold, hard truth is this world is a tough place. This business world is even grittier. Your competitors will constantly jab you until they get the chance to knock you out. But they won't stop there. If you fall to the ground, they continue to stomp you out because there isn't some business referee there to save you.

Even worse than that is when your customers or even your own ex-employees try to hit you with a two-piece combo when you're not looking (and I am not talking about two pieces of chicken and a biscuit, which I am thinking about at this moment). One customer is on Yelp leaving you a bad review for their cold food that they showed up thirty-five minutes late for while one of your prior employees is trashing you on Glassdoor for asking them to work on a Saturday night even when they knew their shift included weekend night work. It may not be fair, but it's how the world is, and you must find a way to win even when the rules are against you. In the business world, people are coming at you from every direction, trying to take their pound of flesh. You must protect your business and brand at all times as they are all gunning for you.

You have to learn that offense can be defense when it comes to marketing, so being two steps ahead is key. Other times, no response is the best response as you don't want to give your enemies energy or material to work with. Don't be the brand that sees a bear trap yet still sticks their arm in it because they think they are too clever to get trapped. Then you're stuck and left with the options to chew your own arm off to escape or becoming someone's dinner. Neither of these options sound wonderful, so let's try to avoid them.

A good example in recent times is when a famous YouTuber made a comment about a company's products. The company said the statements were false and to take them down or it would sue. My first thought is, this is just throwing jet fuel on the fire. You try to leave the legal route out of this conversation until it becomes an imperative. Don't fire up an influencer with a massive following. It will likely cause more damage to your brand than you want.

So what should they have done? The company could have produced its own video demonstrating how all of the claims were wrong. They also could have reached out to the channel to see if they could get together on live video to discuss the concerns. There were many other ways to attack this with a plan to win without causing more damage to the brand. If the company was right and the YouTuber was wrong, this turns into a ton of positive PR and free marketing. Save the heavy-handed tactics for later. Don't be afraid to go to war. People must know not to mess with you, but there is a time and place to do that.

Kane's Straightforward Insight

As marketers, it is our job to be custodians of the brands and companies we represent. After all, if we don't do it, who in our organizations will? But as simple as that idea is, look around at some of the companies and brands operating in your local neighborhood—and you'll be hard-pressed not to find a number of businesses with less-than-stellar reviews and ratings plastered all over Google, Yelp, and whichever other review platform exists in your area. How many times have you stumbled across a local business with an average of a two-star rating having accumulated six reviews over the past five years in operation? Small sample sizes can really hurt businesses that don't invest the requisite time and energy into protecting their brands.

Protecting your brand means doing everything in your power to control the narrative and reputation your business lives in. Contrary to what some believe, protecting your brand isn't hoaxing the public into thinking your brand is something it's not. Instead, it's about gathering a consensus opinion about your company then using those insights to achieve greater reputation over time.

The law of large numbers is one of marketing's good friends. The reality is that customers who leave reviews on ratings platforms typically live on two ends of the happiness spectrum; they're either ecstatic about the service they received or utterly distraught. Customers who think the service they received was "meh" or as expected are the quiet majority. This is why it's so important to harvest as many reviews of your company as possible. Incentivize your customers to leave reviews if you have to. But don't be afraid to gather public opinion about your business.

Between the law of large numbers, mean reversion, and the idea that you will be tapping into the quiet majority, chances are you'll be doing the things you need to protect your brand in both the short and long term. Data exist indicating that review harvesting has an outsized positive effect on revenue for businesses big and small. In fact, businesses that acquired more than twenty-five reviews within the past ninety days of business typically outperform their competitors by some 87 percent on the top line. Add to this the fact that most businesses are well-reviewed—75 percent of businesses have a rating of four stars or above—and you can start to see the pragmatism and practicality of protecting your brand by harvesting the thoughts and experiences of your customers. Tap into the silent majority; chances are they're happier with your business than you think.

36

STEALING CUSTOMERS
IS EXPENSIVE

James's Aggressive Posture

They say crime doesn't pay (tell that to the douches who kept breaking into my childhood home.) Now technically, if you were those guys robbing the houses on my block while littering the sidewalk with the Craftsman tools they dropped while trying to get away, crime likely didn't pay. Nor did it get them onto *Lifestyles of the Rich and Famous* with Robin Leach. In fact, many of them are probably still doing a bid at Jackson Prison in Michigan.

In general, though, stealing is expensive. It costs you either time or money. And in the case of stealing customers, it costs a lot of money. It's generally cheaper to get there first and make people a fan of your product before they ever get a chance to try another one. The last thing you want to do is get to the market late, especially with a new product or service, then have to spend heavily on marketing. It's much easier to be first on the block while everyone is curious rather than trying to entice someone to give your business a try.

Think about your favorite place to eat at. What would it take for you to try something similar down the street? How many times would you have to see a TV commercial or social media ad before you even thought about it? Five to ten times? Think about that CPM and your bank account starts draining fast.

This is our job as growth consultants. Our clients are not always first to market, and, as business owners, we like to roll our sleeves up and get dirty. The key to winning this battle is to have a strategy to win the war; otherwise, the battle never ends. It will take months or likely years to chip away at your competitor's base as you run targeted ads to get them to try you out. You'll lose not only the ad spend but also the promotions you'll run to tempt them to give you a try. If you're late to the market but have an advantage such as price or superior product, you just have to fight until you win the war. Relentless. Unwavering.

Then you hopefully have taken enough business to recoup your investment over the next couple of years. If you're lucky, you put enough pressure to run your competitor right out of business. Many business owners are too busy buying cars and homes in order to get likes. Stay disciplined and keep reinvesting into your business, more marketing, more sales, more everything.

One more thing. You must never give them a reason to try something else. Once you get them in your web, you do what you have to do to keep them there, even if you have to go full-on Kathy Bates in *Misery* (okay, maybe a little aggressive, but bed chains are cheap these days, or so I hear).

So what costs more than stealing customers because you showed up fashionably late to the market? Acquiring the customers, losing them, and having to reacquire them, now that sounds expensive! Let's avoid that. Once you have good customers, do whatever you have to do to keep them. When it comes to marketing strategy, be a wartime general with the relentless pursuit of growth on your mind and you'll win more wars than you lose. But you'll win only if you can protect your battleship, aka your customers.

Kane's Measured Analysis

My first job out of college was as a reporter at a small community newspaper in Boston. I think I made something like fifteen dollars an hour, lived nearly an hour outside of the city center where I worked, and spent far more time on the public transit system than I ever wanted to. Once every so often, however, I used to scrounge up enough in the piggy bank to rent a Mint car (a Zipcar competitor back in the day; do they even exist anymore?) for a day to do a large grocery run and take my girlfriend (my wife now) on a short road trip. My car of choice? An Audi A3 hatchback.

Since those days, I've always wanted my own Audi. When I bought one a few years ago, it was the bookend of a love affair with the brand that started during my time as a broke kid in Boston. I'm such a fan of the Audi brand that I don't really envision myself driving another make of car. Ever.

Why do I bring up this story? Because it speaks to an important marketing lesson. Human beings fall in love with brands just as they do other human beings, pets, hobbies, and whatever else we fall in love with.

Think of your favorite pizza joint that you frequent. How often do you order pizza from another store now that you have a favorite? My guess is rarely.

This is why it's crucial to understand that stealing customers is incredibly expensive. This is because stealing customers requires your company to overcome a number of hurdles, namely capturing the attention of the potential customer and then crossing the chasm such that the potential customer departs from their current brand preferences and tries your product or service instead. Business, especially in small markets, is really a zero-sum game. Consumers have a certain level of disposable income they are willing to spend on food, drink, or entertainment. Your brand is competing not only with the companies that sell a similar product to yours, but also with every other expenditure in a consumer's wallet. People don't have unlimited money, after all.

You could line up the fanciest European, American, and Japanese cars, with the best specs, the most horsepower, the best sound system, and whatever else makes a great car, and I would still probably choose to go with an Audi. Which brings me to another important marketing principle: don't give your customers a reason to try another brand! Once we have a captive customer, it's our job as marketers to think of every and any way possible to keep that customer engaged. Don't take customer loyalty for granted. The hardest thing to do is to acquire a new customer and make them stick. Remember stealing customers from other brands is expensive—focus on acquiring new ones and keeping them, at (nearly) all costs.

37

ORGANIC SEARCH RULES THE WORLD

James's Direct Discussion

I remember the day we went all in on organic search. Back around 2007, a Seth Godin video was posted on YouTube. He was giving a presentation at Google, telling Google employees about how good Google is. Really? Sounds like your modern-day management consultant. Seth was spitting that Marty Kaan shit from *House of Lies*. At the time, it was eye-opening and led us down the path that would be an ever-winding road for over fifteen years.

It was so simple. Whether it's organic search or paid AdWords, Google puts things in front of you that you're looking for. Simple, right? If I am searching for toasters, Google serves me toasters. Perfect! This was the breakthrough difference from traditional media and marketing such as billboards, TV, magazines, and radio. You may spend $5,000 on a radio ad to market toasters and only 1 percent of the listeners are in the market for toasters. Doesn't sound very efficient, right? This is where search engines changed the whole game.

Now we can talk about paid ads on search engines at a later time as we want to focus on organic search. In our experience, those who find our websites organically have a much higher conversation rate than paid ads. This is why it makes sense to go all in on organic or have a mixed mode of focus on organic and paid.

They say the rich get richer because they make money when they are not working. This is how I view organic search, websites, and other online content in general. People can find you around the clock, in any time zone, at any place on the planet. You can be asleep on vacation in Bali and someone in Nebraska has just found your business in a search engine and is filling out a contact form. Money never sleeps and neither does your website. Essentially, all forms of online content can be a lead generator, from videos on YouTube to written content on Medium or a podcast on Spotify. Put as many traps there as you can so more and more people can find you.

Sometimes we have to do the hard things to win. It seems easier to throw money at problems in this day and age, but it may not yield the results you want. Sure you can run that radio ad for $5,000 and now it's off your plate, but will it yield the same results as creating eight to ten new pieces of content a month for your website? We likely know the answer, but it just seems like a lot more work to do all of that writing.

While there is only limited space at the top of the search results where only the top five to ten search results matter, overall space is infinite. There is no limit to the amount of content you can have, so stuff the search engines full like you do your belly on Thanksgiving. Keep creating until people can find you a thousand different ways and your business will begin to grow. But remember as time goes on, if anyone can do it, they'll ruin it. One day organic search may not be the unlock, so have a Plan B.

Kane's Approachable Take

When was the last time you found what you were looking for on the second page of Google (or any search engine, for that matter)? It's been reported that up to 92 percent of search traffic clicks is captured by the first page of Google, with more than a quarter of those clicks going to the number one ranked result. That's incredible visibility and a real competitive advantage when it comes to choking the supply of business to competitors in a crowded marketplace. In that sense, depending on the margins on your product or service, there may be no better ROI tactic than to do whatever it takes to get the number one ranking on Google. Unfortunately, many marketers know just how valuable this digital real estate is and search engine marketing is as saturated a battleground as they come.

Frankly, James is the best search engine marketer I've ever met. I've watched him leverage search engine marketing to build multiple nine-figure valuation companies through impressive multi-brand and flanker brand strategies. Before meeting and working with James, it would have been challenging to convince me you could build a sustainable competitive advantage via search engine marketing, but over time, I've seen James's companies continue to grow without a heady amount of investment, purely off the back of the compounding effects of great search engine marketing and operational excellence.

So how can you make search engine marketing work for you even when the playing field is so crowded you feel like you're in the Tokyo subway during rush hour? Start by finding long-tail, lower competition keywords that you can build a lot of content around on your website. Don't be impatient and think your brand-new website is going to capture any ranking credit at the start—especially for high-volume keywords that everyone wants to rank for. Use search engine marketing tools like SEM Rush or Moz to find keywords that can bring in tens to hundreds of visitors for terms that are peripheral to the core content of your product or service, and slowly build a catalog of articles, videos, and informative content on your website such that it becomes a hub for enthusiasts of your product or service. Pair this tactic up with some good PR and backlink generation, and you've got a playbook that will work over time. Organic search is hard, but it works. And from a pure lead and revenue generation standpoint, I've yet to come across a traffic source that works better.

38

AUTHENTICITY & KEEPING IT ONE HUNDRED

Kane's Sound Reflection

In a world as noisy and crowded as the one we are all living in, authenticity is the secret sauce that allows businesses to cut through the noise and connect deeply with their audience. Customers can detect inauthenticity, and it can have a lasting impact on their trust and loyalty toward a business. Authenticity is more than just a buzzword; it's the core principle of a sustainable, successful business.

Take the example of Gap. In 2010, the global retail giant decided to change its iconic logo, a move that came out of the blue and wasn't aligned with what the brand stood for. The response was immediate and overwhelmingly negative. Loyal customers felt alienated and confused. The authenticity Gap had built over the years, the familiarity and trust, seemed to have been tossed aside. Gap reversed the decision within a week, but the damage was done. This example is a stark reminder of the cost of abandoning one's roots and authenticity.

Another example is New Coke. In the mid-1980s, Coca-Cola, one of the world's most iconic brands, attempted to rebrand its classic recipe under the name New Coke. The result was a spectacular failure. Consumers rejected the new taste and the brand's image suffered a significant blow. The move wasn't just a change in product; it felt like a betrayal of the authenticity Coca-Cola had cultivated for nearly a century. The company had to reintroduce the old formula under the name Coca-Cola Classic to regain customer trust.

These examples illustrate the consequences of neglecting authenticity. Authenticity is rooted in understanding who you are as a brand and what you stand for. It's about remaining true to your mission, values, and brand personality, regardless of changing market trends. It's about consistent messaging, from advertising to customer service to product development.

Businesses that maintain their authenticity are more likely to foster deeper relationships with their customers. An authentic brand offers something real and tangible, and customers appreciate this. A brand that stays true to its core principles instills a sense of trust and loyalty in its customers.

Look at brands like Patagonia, Apple, and Tesla. They have remained unwaveringly true to their mission and values over the years and their authenticity is evident. Patagonia is committed to environmental responsibility, Apple to design and innovation, and Tesla to electric mobility and sustainable energy. They don't just claim these values; they live by them in every aspect of their business. As a result, their customers feel a deeper connection with these brands, turning them into loyal advocates.

In conclusion, authenticity is a business's true north. It's not about jumping on the latest trend or making drastic changes to fit in. It's about understanding who you are, what you stand for, and remaining true to that, come what may. Authenticity may seem like an intangible concept, but its impact is very tangible in the form of loyal customers, a strong brand reputation, and long-term business success. As a business, it pays to be genuine. It pays to be you.

James's Hard-Charging Insight

This insight hit me one day after I walked into a sporting goods store for the outdoors lifestyle. It seemed like I had just walked into another normal sporting goods store I knew. It had the same style, layout, and feel, just different colors and maybe some random camo thrown in here and there. It had the same poor service on the floor, but it was even worse because many of those on the floor had no idea what they were talking about. It was like walking into one of those giant hardware and lumber stores where no one ever seems to know anything about anything. It didn't seem like they fished, or hunted, or had ever camped in a tent. It just seemed fake. Almost faker than fake, essentially a whole gang of outdoors posers trying to sell you stuff.

And, yeah, they didn't make it. The store was often dead. Even during the holiday season, the parking lot wouldn't be packed. This goes back to another chapter in this book: your customers are not as stupid as you think. As the saying goes, real recognize real.

To no one's surprise, people would rather drive an extra ten- to fifteen-minutes to the more authentic store. Think about it. Imagine you want to take your kid fishing and you have never fished. You walk into a store to get product recommendations on fishing gear, but the sales rep doesn't know anything about fishing either. Now what would go wrong here?

As a customer, you would be better off watching a couple of YouTube videos on fishing and taking a random guess on what to buy. This is a common complaint amongst many of the brick and mortar stores in this day and age. Even if the brand is authentic, they can't get the proper staff to complete the experience.

When building your brand, you have to think about what your customers will value the most. This takes a deep understanding of your average customer's buying habits. For example, there are numerous national Mexican restaurant chains that do very well, but you wouldn't create a brand like that to target those looking for authentic Mexican food. Even then authentic Mexican food may not have the brand aesthetic we once thought. You could do authentic Mexican food in a modern store build out, for example. Where I came from, if they didn't have a mariachi band on a Friday night, you would go out of business.

What's an eye opener on the sporting goods store is that they sold many of the same products the more authentic store did. Yet people still drove further to shop the place that seemed more real. Customers simply didn't want to fork over their hard-earned dollars to the cookie-cutter retail place. In a world where everything comes in a strip mall like a build-a-boy-band in five easy steps, consumers are saying we don't want that. Who does?

39

MARKET GAPS, QUICK STACKS OF CASH

James's Unfiltered Assessment

To give you my ad hoc Cliff Notes of a Sun Tzu quote, I'll say this: if your opponent gives you an opening, move at the speed of shotgunning a beer. That may not be the most eloquent way to say it, but you get the point. Every day in business is just another day of war with your enemies. If you're slow, a faster apex predator will chase you down and chew you up like dim sum on a Friday evening. Your goal at the bare minimum is to always be a worthy opponent but more ideally, the victor.

In the business world, we spend a lot of time looking for new markets to create, the type of blue ocean strategies that soon-to-be billionaires dream of. But within all markets are gaps. It's goddamn expensive to create a new market, but a metric ton of money can be made from finding gaps within those already established markets, especially ancillary markets for established products and services.

Once you find that gap, make sure you get there first and cement yourself into a solid footing. The last thing you want to do is discover a market gap only to let a competitor catch wind of it and take their own little tranche while you're slowly ramping up. Let them get a small enough piece of the pie to choke on, but that's about it. Your goal is dominate this mini market segment as fast as possible.

Now you must do the research and make sure the gap is big enough. What is the maximize size of this market within a market? If you get only 25 percent of this market, will that be worth it? You cannot assume others won't come after you. They will, as we live in a world with infinite competition. Make sure the market gap is big enough not even Evel Knievel could jump it.

You can find market gaps in different ways. For example, traditional insurance companies are not always the ideal place to get insurance for a classic car. There's insurance companies just for classic cars now. Another way to find these submarkets is to look at products or services that need to be augmented so as to make the product more user-friendly. For example, the paper towel company sells paper towels, but they are easier to use when you have a paper towel dispenser. Many companies make paper towel dispensers for homes that are fixed or bulky, but what if you need one for an RV, a boat, or events? I mentioned this because I just bought something like this as I needed something portable.

As I am writing this, I have the TV on for background noise. One of those commercials just came on for dating-over-fifty apps—another market gap someone found. Now, if you try to create a dating app for left-handed sous-chefs in Ohio, that venture may not work out so well. Again, find a gap that has a real need with a market size that is worth going after, and it will all fall into place.

Kane's Considered Take

Market gaps are interesting to marketers because, on one hand, they represent opportunity and, on the other, they could be areas of false promise. Is there a market gap because other firms have tried and failed? Or is there a market gap because there hasn't been a product or service with your specific blend of capabilities? Those are the important questions to ask yourself when looking at market gaps.

As a marketer, you're taught to analyze business landscapes through the lens of the three C's—customer, company, and competition. Who is the customer, what are your company's unique competitive advantages and capabilities, and what does the competition look like? Market gaps appear when you find target customers who are not serviced by an existing product or service. Low-competition spaces are a great place for a marketer to try to capture business.

A fascinating recent example of market gap exploitation is Meta—formerly Facebook—and the company's strategic move into the metaverse. Facebook was arguably one of the most successful business concepts of the past couple of decades. On the surface, there was very little need to pivot or rock the ship. But they did—revamping the entire company's brand and transitioning into a company more focused on building the future of the metaverse than investing in its existing, highly profitable ads business.

Why? The executive team at Meta sees a market gap, an opportunity to build a customer base early in a space that has low competition and a high barrier to entry. The idea of the metaverse has many definitions, and Meta is looking to add its own utilitarian version of a metaverse to the business lexicon—and redefine a category. You can argue that the branding change was catalyzed by other factors, like the mounting legal and societal pressures the company is facing with regard to its business model and privacy stance, but that's a topic for another conversation.

While it's too early to judge Meta's plan to develop its metaverse business, it's clear the opportunity to exploit a market gap has the potential to be either an enormous success, the kind that commentators would hail as genius, or an enormous bust, a multibillion-dollar mistake and destruction of shareholder value. That's the message I want to hone in on when it comes to market gaps. Market gaps are fascinating for marketers because they represent opportunity. But they're like mirages in the desert. They may or may not actually be there in the end.

40

THE AWARENESS PHASE
OF MARKETING

James's Inventive Approach

Bringing new products and services to the market is one of the most difficult things to do in marketing. Not only is it hard to bring new products to
market, keeping them there and profitable is a whole other problem. My
process in the past was really a three-phase setup, and I'm talking about
wiring up power here.

Each of the three phases serves its own purpose depending on the life
cycle of the product. We start with the awareness phase, which this chapter will focus on. It's an annoy-them-until-they-buy approach that has an
initial no to low ROI and climbs up throughout phase one. Phase two is
the reminder phase. The market is aware of your product; consumers just
need to see a little something to plant that seed as it's easy to get lost the
noise these days. Phase three is the recovery phase. The market stopped
caring about you, so how do you become cool and relevant again?

Let's talk about phase one. A well-known sandwich shop comes out with a new sandwich every so often. Do they launch the product and hope their customers see it when they come in for lunch? Hell no they don't. It often begins with billboards. You'll be driving around and see this new sandwich and pay it no mind. A couple of days later, you'll see it on another billboard. And once again you'll see it on another billboard a few days later, or this could all happen in one day if they bought out a metro area.

The seed is planted in your head now; it just needs water. If someone asked if you heard about the new sandwich, you would say yes as you have a familiarity now with the product. This is the "no- to low-ROI" part of phase one as you haven't bought anything yet.

Now it's Saturday afternoon and you turn on the TV. The new sandwich commercial pops up with the sound of sizzling bacon with cheese melting and leaking off the side. It's food porn at it's finest and now you're starting to think maybe you should try this. But you don't, not yet anyway. The seed was just watered.

A week goes by and you're driving home from work. The new sandwich radio ad pops up taking about how great this would be for dinner. You're thinking to yourself this indeed would be good for dinner! Off you go to try the new sandwich.

The awareness phase isn't fast or cheap. They say in sales it takes about seven touches for someone to buy your product or service. Sure, there are outliers who see the first ad and run out and buy it, but it usually takes multiple touches through two or three different types of media to get the consumer to purchase. For example, if you're making cold calls to sell a professional service, you may have to speak with the prospect three or four times, send two or three emails with marketing collateral plus some other form of media such as PR, social media, or even traditional media. You hope someone did the math and figured out it would take fifteen dollars in ad spend to get someone to buy a sandwich and if they come back four times in sixty days, it's worth it. I'm making up numbers here, but you get the point. To bring a new product to market, you likely need a budget and a lot of patience, but keep grinding; there is no cheap and easy way to complete this phase.

Kane's Measured Reflection

Marketing's role during the launch of a new product or service is to make the target market (and ideally those outside of it) aware of its existence. After all, it's very hard to sell something nobody knows anything about, let alone don't know they need.

James came up with a very clever framework for new products and services years ago that is as evergreen as frameworks get. The beauty of the three-part framework is that, for marketing practitioners, it's very easy to identify which area of the framework you are currently operating within and to understand what your product or service needs at that very moment.

The first step of the three-part framework is the awareness phase—it is a marketer's job to drive as much awareness and hype toward a product or service as humanly possible. The more eyeballs you get on your new product and service, the better. And better can be defined on several fronts.

The first, of course, is the potential for revenue. The more people are aware of what you've just brought to market, the more opportunity you have of actually selling the thing. The second is greater opportunity for feedback. It's foolish to think you can bring a product or service to market and expect it to be 100 percent perfect to what your target demographic wants and needs. Feedback is crucial to iterating your product or service in its most utilitarian form.

Practically speaking, however, the awareness phase is often the most costly phase of the three-part framework. During the awareness phase, you are working on establishing a benchmark for your customer acquisition cost, and the only way to establish a number here is to acquire customers at a cost. Getting an idea of how efficient your marketing can be when acquiring new customers is great because it allows you to build out an estimate for CLV, which in turn enables you to make an educated calculation for profitability over time.

This is why the awareness phase is so important when bringing new products and services to market. Not only is it an opportunity to get eyeballs and potential leads looking at your new innovation, but it is the start of building an analytics framework that allows you to make data-driven decisions around your product and marketing going forward.

One of the biggest mistakes I see small business owners make all the time is not understanding the unit economics of their businesses. It's one thing to guess at the contribution margin of your product, but it's a completely different ball game when you understand how much it costs to acquire a new customer, what their lifetime value is, and how much you can spend going forward to acquire every marginal customer. Understanding your unit economics allows you to make appropriate decisions around scale—the goal of any business that wants to land among the stars. It all starts during the awareness phase.

41

THE REMINDER PHASE
OF MARKETING

James's Spirited Outlook

Welcome to phase two. Please sign this waiver and watch your step. We are not responsible for injury due to equipment failure or lost and stolen items. Pickpockets are common in this area, so please hold on to your valuables. That's pretty much the disclaimer that should come with any launch of a new company, product, or service. Since we were talking sandwiches, we will keep that theme going.

So you tried that new sandwich a few times and now you're over it. Like most things in this world, the newness wears off quicker than last night's Tinder date. Mix that in with the culture in America of loving fads and you can see why we lose interest in things at a rapid pace.

Just as you're getting tired of that sandwich, you open your social media and boom! There is a new sandwich from a different place. And another ad for a chicken wing joint. Oh, no! A taco truck is near me too?

What?? Taaaccooos! You're bombarded with endless emails, social media, TV ads, and billboards. It is nonstop. There is so much noise out there, it's hard to break through to people and, even when you do, trying to keep them interested is sometimes even harder. At the end of the day, your competitors are the pickpockets, taking your customers attention away one quick snatch and grab at a time.

There is no "set it and forget it" when it comes to keeping consumers deep in your brand. Very few companies get to enjoy that. You rarely see a Chipotle commercial, for example; they had a cult following, including myself who would eat there four or five times a week. Now they are running commercials as the market is shifting beneath their feet. The truth is, once you fall out of a habit, you simply forget about it. Not to mention, there is now a hundred food options between my home and the nearest Chipotle. There is infinite competition out there.

Part of the lesson here is don't wait for demand to fade before you start reminding your customers. That weekly email I get from Jimmy Johns is all I need to get that Italian sandwich a couple of times a month, for example. Social media used to work, but as a brand, you can get 500,000 followers yet your post makes it to only 5,000. The algorithm owns us, so the days of free exposure are almost over. We are right back to breaking out your pocketbook. Think about how insane that is. You essentially have to run ads to reach the people who already follow you. At that point I am taking that ad spend to TV or somewhere else.

By waiting for demand to slow, you'll find out it is already too late. Now it will take more money to get them back as you go into the recovery phase, which we will talk about next. Keep them knee deep in your brand with a weekly email or text with a deal, create a loyalty program as an incentive to buy more often, and never stop advertising even if it means putting things on a trickle budget. That's a good one actually, NSA, Never Stop Advertising. The big chains with the big ad spend have figured this out. They never stop marketing to you. It's endless. They never allow you to forget their brand. Even when the budget is tight, find a way to stay in the customer's face or you face being the forgotten brand.

Kane's Sensible Take

The second phase of the three-part framework is the reminder phase—this is what most consumers think about when they think about marketing and brand building. The Delta ads you see when you're traveling through airports, the McDonalds ads you see during the World Cup, and the Starbucks ads you see on billboards when you're traveling down the interstate are all examples of businesses executing on the reminder phase of business building.

Once your small business is up and running and you've learned—from customer feedback and/or sales—that your idea is gaining traction and you're finding product-market fit, the next step to growth and brand building is to invest in reminding the world your product or service exists. Now is the time to pour fuel on the fire.

Ask yourself why, despite being a world-famous brand, Coca-Cola still feels the need to advertise at every major sporting event that happens across the globe. Why do UberEats and DoorDash run advertising when basically anybody with a cellphone probably already has both apps on their phones? Why do car companies like Buick and BMW advertise constantly on television?

The answer is in the way the human brain works. We're forgetful and we are more like squirrels than we'd like to think, always chasing the newest shiny object. Big brands win because they pour a big portion of their profits into reminding customers they exist, so the next time we make a purchasing decision in their segments, no other brands come to mind.

This is even more important for brands and companies operating in hypercompetitive spaces. Think commodities, where brand is important but price even more so. Think spaces, where you make purchasing decisions frequently, like where you are going to get lunch today. If your small business is operating in a segment or space where you want customers to choose you frequently and there is a lot of competition and variety then reminding potential consumers that you exist is crucial. Remind. Remind. Remind. That's all advertising is once you get your brand off the ground and have achieved some awareness. Don't give your competitors any room to breathe.

42
THE DREADED RECOVERY PHASE

James's Tenacious Assessment

The next chapter title popped up and my first thought was Eminem's album, Recovery, which I have decided to play while I write this chapter. And yes, it is a different kind of recovery. I just enjoyed this album and I usually write with music in the background. Music is energy, so consuming music gives you fuel in a way.

Anyway, let's hop into phase three. You have launched a new company, product, or service. You have annoyed your customers with a media blitz and advertising campaign until they finally relented and bought. They started to slip away and you either didn't take action soon enough to stay in front of them or, even worse, you didn't stay in front of them at all. So now they are long gone. The good news is, you're not starting from ground zero. You do have some brand equity left in the hearts and minds of the consumer. But how do you bring them back?

The natural thing to do is market again. You hit them with a deal in email or on social media. Maybe you run a radio ad or a TV commercial promoting the deal. It's a place to start and it's better than doing nothing. The problem here is, once someone falls out of love with you, there is no amount of roses or drugstore chocolates that will make them love you again. Once it's gone, it's usually gone for good. That's a lesson you hopefully learned early in life and didn't repeat the same mistake twice. It's just time to move on to something new because that is what they are seeking.

The key here is "new". We love new; it's fresh, it's unknown, it's a good feeling to try something new. If you're going to spend the money to get old customers back, you may as well launch something new. Don't bring them back for the same old thing you have been selling over and over. Give them a few looks at a new offering. Look, you're going to spend the time or money either way. Do you want to spend it on promoting legacy products or something new? If you see a TV ad for the sandwich you have been eating for five years, you'll just tune it out. But if a commercial comes on for a new ten-hour smoked BBQ brisket sandwich with oodles of Tillamook cheese, on it, well, hey, hey there, you have my attention now.

Now we have come full circle as we are right back to the awareness phase. How fun was this! You're back to launching a new product or service and you're looking for ways to entice buyers to try it out. The only difference here is, once again, you have some brand equity to work with. Hopefully you were saving all of those email addresses from online orders. If you do wide net marketing such as a TV campaign, you should know what channels your average customer watches. Through this process, you will have the chance to bring back old customers and attract new customers with your exciting new product launch. There are some synergies here.

To wrap this up and to blend it all together like one of those green sludge health drinks at a smoothie joint, I'll say this: Never stop advertising and constantly innovate. Never put yourself in the position of needing a recovery phase. If you're also looking for the next big thing to sell, that means you're always thinking about how to grow the business. Complacency is the death rattle for all companies. Don't let yourself fall victim to this one.

Kane's Grounded Viewpoint

The third and final stage of the three-part framework is recovery—an interesting title and an interesting phase of business, especially for small businesses with a constant push and pull of resource constraints. The recovery phase of the three-part framework happens when your prospects become desensitized to the advertising and marketing you have done during the reminder phase. Remind, remind, remind—remember that part? Well, at some point, you get customers to buy enough that they start looking for other options. After all, human beings like variety. Can you imagine eating the same food every single day? At some point, you will start to look elsewhere for a bit of a change.

The issue, however, is that looking for an alternative becomes a one-time thing, then a two-time thing, and, before you know it, you've lost the customer for good. The loyalty is no longer there and the customer is prone to get hooked on another company's product or service.

The recovery phase is activated when you, as a small business practitioner, work to bring back former customers. How? The mechanisms can be different, but the key is to innovate. This is why there is so much menu innovation at the big fast-food establishments—they are aware that after a while, you will get bored with the Big Mac and try the Whopper next door. How do they bring you back? By bringing back the McRib for a limited time only.

You need to do this at your business too. Innovate such that you can bring something new to the market. This gets everyone excited, which should remind you of the awareness phase! And that's the whole point of the three-part framework. The goal of the framework is to loop your marketing efforts so you know when and where to spend your resources. By bringing new products to the market and bringing back the excitement around your brand, you are activating the recovery phase—which then kick-starts the loop back to the start of the process. You are reactivating your old customers while catching the eye of new customers—growing your business over time. The engine has begun. Your snowball is rolling downhill.

43

WHAT THE HELL IS IT THAT YOU DO?

James's Unabashed Insight

If you have ever watched a TV commercial and thought, "That was cool, but what in the hell do they do?" you're not alone. This happens on websites all the time. You stumble around this vaguely interesting site, you're reading the "about" page and their "what we do" section has a lot of text, but it doesn't say what they do. You know what you need, but you cannot figure out if this company is who you need.

Why is this so complicated? In this case, some companies hire a web developer and say, "Build me a website!" The issue here is the same person laying the lines of code isn't always the best person to design the graphics. And the people who lay the code and design the graphics are not always the best ones to write all of the content for your website. It takes a team to build a solid-looking brand with well-articulated content.

A very simple example is business cards, not that anyone even uses them anymore. Having my title on my card was paramount to me, not for the vanity of it all, believe it or not. The title on the card allows a stranger to remember what in the hell you exactly do when they pull that card out six months from now. Think back to how many times you met someone and they gave you a card and you forgot what they did. Were they in sales? Are they a CFO? Did they work in the supply chain? Sure, you can Google them or look on LinkedIn, but back in the day, that title allowed you to simply explain what it is you do.

There isn't much value in being mysterious when it comes to your branding. You're not some underground EDM DJ like when everyone was trying to figure out who Mala was, which created extra buzz. The reality is, if your TV commercial or social media ad or website cannot quickly and efficiently communicate what it is you do, people bounce and forget you. Even if you do it right, it will still be overlooked. A great example is a career services company I own that does résumé writing, outplacement, and career coaching. We have résumé writing all over the place on the website, on the main pages, in the menu titles, page titles, and contact pages. Yet every day someone will contact us and ask, "Do you write résumés?" Even when we try to make it clear as hell, they still look right past it!

Never underestimate the consumer's lack of attention to detail. Make your brand messaging clear. Spell out what exactly it is you do, who you help, and what you sell and why. If you're a home builder, you say you build homes. Don't mask your business as a construction company, a general contractor, or a home designer. If you do all of those things, say that, but make sure the clearest message is that you're a home builder. If you say you're a construction company, you may leave people asking what kind of construction. Do they build office buildings? Roads? What do they do? See how this could turn into a mess quickly?

If you landed on a home builder's page that said above the fold, "We build homes in the Austin, Texas, area," you would get the point, right? Spell it out. Communicate what you do as clearly as possible, and you will generate sales leads, lower your bounce rate, and increase conversions.

Kane's Sensible Stance

Clarity in marketing is important. Customers are busy and they don't have time to fumble around your company's website looking for the information they need. I believe it's Mark Cuban who said you want to make the sale as frictionless as possible. And it's true. Customers have so many options nowadays that if you're not delivering the information they need to make a decision quickly, they will move on to a new option faster than you can say, "wait, wait…".

Rookie marketers are prone to the error of under-elaboration on company websites. There are so many weird and wonderful website templates out there, it's easy to start dreaming about building the slickest, most esoteric website for your small business that sells garden hoses. "Let's have an image slide in here and another abstract element slide in over top of that image, and a graphic of a hose twist and wind its way up the side of the screen …"

Have you landed on a cool website but after minutes of looking around were still befuddled by what they even do? I have, and digital marketing firms are arguably the most guilty of this. Many an agency has developed visually stunning websites that say nothing at all. And even if you were in the market for digital marketing services, you end up leaving the website after pulling your hair out trying to find the email address to reach out to.

This is why clarity and simplicity are virtues when it comes to branding and marketing your small business. Make clear, right at the top of your website, what it is you do and how you alleviate a specific pain point for your ideal customer. Then make your contact information as easy to find as humanly possible. Stick your company's toll-free number right in the navigation of your site if you have to. Create a link that opens up a contact form that is as easy to use as possible. Hell, throw a pop-up over the top of the screen after eight seconds in order to capture your prospects' contact information. Make everything simple and easy.

Simplicity and clarity is also important when thinking about what to name your company. There is a time and place for more obscure, abstract naming schemes. But for most small businesses, sticking to simple and memorable brand names is the best way to create brand equity and customer recognition. As I write this, a mattress company named after a fruit is advertising on television. Unless the mattress is made of that fruit, this makes no sense. Keep things simple, memorable, and relevant.

44

NEW RESTAURANT, OLD RESTAURANT

James's Robust View

The first time this concept crossed my mind was when I watched Walgreens build a new location right next to an old Rite Aid. I was like, "Holy shit. These guys have the audacity to build right next door." Well, technically, I think it was across the street, but you get the point.

I was probably in my early twenties when this first happened, but I've seen it again and again over the years as these turf wars were happening. When I say turf wars, it's kind of like when you read about motorcycle gangs beating each other up with hammers outside of Starbucks. I use that story a lot, as you well know by now. They were fighting over control of a couple of city blocks. At times, this feels like what Walgreens was doing to other people or what you see Lowe's trying to do with Home Depot. The thing is, you rarely witnessed Rite Aid go out of business, and come to find out Lowe's and Home Depot can both thrive in the same location at the same time if the population is dense enough.

The lesson came to reality when I saw this happen with restaurants. Even if there was enough population density, oftentimes the new restaurant would take such a large cut out of the old restaurant next door it would run them out of business.

I learned that lesson probably about fifteen years ago when I took a business strategy concept to an MBA professor at Michigan State University. Someone I interviewed mentioned a class on crazy strategies. I have an overly aggressive / let's take it to the streets business mentality, so this was exciting to me. I contacted the professor and gave him a quick rundown of what I was trying to achieve with this particular strategy. He invited me to the campus. I had a multi-brand strategy designed to suck the life out of the market and almost have a monopoly if it was fully executed. For about thirty minutes, as we drank black coffee out of little Styrofoam cups, he kept telling me how it wasn't going to work. About thirty-one minutes in, his whole posture and demeanor changed.

He looked up at me and said, "This is going to work."

My lesson that day was I didn't have to take 100 percent of my competitor's business to win. I just have to take enough business to the point they feel like it's no longer worth it to operate. We figured that's probably 30 or 40 percent. Take away all of their profit and it's game over. Within two years of executing our strategy locally, we had one of our top competitors going out of business. The most satisfying part of that is, one of those business owners actually applied to work for us. If you ever wanted to know how I feel about competing in business, now you know: because I love the win.

That's essentially what happens with restaurants. Large franchises make you set aside money for a remodel down the road. You have likely witnessed a McDonald's or Burger King that looked fine to you, but they tore it down anyway. They have a budget set aside for years that once they get to a certain point, they're going to have to tear it down and build a brand-new one with the new style to keep customers coming back.

Most single-operator restaurants don't do that. To be honest, most of the small business owners I know are too busy spending all their money buying new Range Rovers and fourth homes. They're not saving money for that remodel or a rainy day. Next thing you know, someone moves in with a new restaurant with a new style and new food. Everything's brand-new, clean, and bright. This cuts off a big chunk of their old business and they have no money saved up to do a remodel or to invent a new menu to compete.

You must keep reinvesting in yourself. If you're not trying to put yourself out of business with a new model or business, then don't plan on being here fifty years from now. You have to be ambidextrous in a sense, where you're still doing business the old way, but you're also looking to the future and doing business in a new way. If not that, create a completely new business. If you're not trying to put yourself out of business with something new, your chances of survival are very low. Never stop reinvesting in yourself, stay creative, and keep planning for five to ten years down the road. If you're lucky, there's enough room in the market for everyone. But when that new place comes to town, do you really want to find out then?

Kane's Pragmatic Approach

When you're considering entering a market, it's easy to feel intimidated by established competition. You might think, "The market is already saturated. How can I possibly succeed?" This fear, while understandable, might be steering you away from an opportunity. Think about it in terms of an old restaurant and a new one.

Consider a long-standing restaurant in a bustling neighborhood. It has a loyal clientele, a well-worn menu, and a deep history in the community. Now, you decide to open a new restaurant just down the street. Some may call this decision audacious or even reckless. I'd argue it's neither. Let's dissect why.

The world is a vast place bursting with diverse tastes. Not every customer will be satisfied by the old restaurant's offerings, no matter how tried and true they may be. There's always room for variation, innovation, and new ways of doing things. In short, there's enough of the proverbial pie for everyone.

The first lesson here is don't let existing competition scare you away. Yes, it's daunting to enter a market already populated with businesses that have brand recognition and a customer base. But remember the mere existence of these businesses proves there's a demand for your product or service. And there's always a segment of the market waiting for a fresh, new approach.

Now, on to the second lesson, which revolves around understanding the economics of your business and your competition. If you're going to set up shop in an old market, you need to know the ins and outs of the industry. Understand the unit economics that underpin the competition.

What are their margins? What's their cost structure? This is crucial because it will help you carve out your niche and decide just how much market share you need to capture to make your competitors falter.

Let's go back to our restaurant analogy. Perhaps the old restaurant has high overhead costs due to an oversized dining room, leading to slim margins. In response, you design your restaurant with a smaller dining area supplemented by robust takeout and delivery services. By understanding the unit economics of the old restaurant, you can build your own with a competitive edge, thereby taking a bite out of their market share.

The world is big enough for the old restaurant and your new one. In business, it's not always about reinventing the wheel. Sometimes, it's about making a slightly better wheel or a different kind of wheel that appeals to a new set of customers. So don't be discouraged by a saturated market. Instead, use your understanding of business economics, your unique value proposition, and a healthy dose of ambition to carve out your piece of the market pie.

Remember markets aren't really zero-sum games. You don't need to take over the whole world. You just need to find your corner of it, serve your customers well, and enjoy the fruits of your labor. In time, your new restaurant might become the old restaurant, giving way to the cycle of innovation and competition in the beautiful ebb and flow of the business world.

45

DO SOMETHING WORTH TALKING ABOUT

James's Bold Outlook

Since I started my first company as a teenager, I have learned valuable lessons. Many of them were obvious, such as you're probably not going to get a business loan if you have no revenue. Another lesson is that it's difficult to get sales without customers. One of those lessons I wasn't prepared for back in the day was how difficult it is to get PR and earned media.

Not only is it difficult, you'll also find out it's a gigantic waste of money unless you have something that is PR-worthy. Public relations firms charge a metric ton of cash—back-up-the-Brinks-truck, stick-your-hands-up kind of cash. Many of them quote, if you're lucky, on the low side, a $5,000 a month retainer. Some of them will go up to $25,000 a month or more depending on the scope. They're crafty enough to never really make any promises. They'll say things like, "Hey, we can't make a news outlet pick your story up," which is 100 percent true.

You'll learn quickly that as you're burning $10,000 a month and you think whatever new sale you want to promote is newsworthy, it just isn't. And that's really the meat of the lesson, thirty-two-ounce tomahawk off-a-wood-fire-grill type of meat. So ask yourself before you jump in with both feet: do you have something that's newsworthy?

No one cares about your sale, your new website, or your new office. There's so much noise out there with social media there's probably a million posts going out per minute across all the platforms. Then, on top of it, companies just like yours have hired countless PR people all around the world to fight for that little bit of space on a website or within a news segment.

So what do you have that is newsworthy? Alright, so you don't have anything that's newsworthy. Now what? If you don't have news, you need some sort of high credibility. One of the fastest ways to get picked up in PR is to have actually done something noteworthy.

So it's cool if you have a PhD who will help you out if they need an authority on a topic. Some of the things that we have witnessed work the best is if you have a published book, even better if the book is a bestseller.

Have you been on TV before, such as reality TV, or featured in some show as an expert? Any nomination for larger or more well-known awards is great, but not that easy to attain. Have you received a large amount of funding for a business or have you sold a business? Maybe you have hundreds of thousands or millions of followers on social media. Now, funnily enough, it's typically hard for unknown businesses to get a lot of followers, but it's not always that hard for an individual. All right, maybe it's a little bit hard, but it is feasible. In a strange way in this new world, somehow major publications and news outlets care more about the number of followers you have than whether or not you have a PhD or a bestselling book.

So as we say, it's always easier to do PR if you've actually done something. To be honest, what it really comes down to is that most modern-day media want a built-in audience such as fans of your book, music, TV show, or your social media content. As newspapers have gone out of business, TV viewership is down and everything's going to an online model. All of these media outlets benefit if you can bring an audience with you.

So if you haven't done something such as publish a book or somehow ended up with a Grammy nomination or didn't go back and get that PhD, what's your next best option? Figure out how to accomplish a high goal that makes your opinion extremely valuable. Or build the biggest audience you can so you have a built-in audience, which is the ultimate incentive for a media outlet to pick up your quote or your interview.

Kane's Reasoned Approach

There's no denying that PR is a powerful tool in a business's marketing arsenal. It has the power to elevate your brand's visibility, validate your value proposition, and create a buzz that resonates with both current and potential customers. But for small businesses, especially those with limited resources or without a major differentiating factor, it can often feel like climbing a steep hill. The solution to this is simple yet profound: do something worth talking about because PR, in essence, becomes easier once you have done something.

Let me explain. We're not merely talking about launching a new product or opening another store—though those can be worthy of PR in their own right. We're talking about creating a story, an event, or a cause, something that's inherently newsworthy and aligns with your brand's values. It's about doing something compelling that warrants attention and sets you apart from the competition.

For instance, you own a local organic food store. Rather than merely promoting your latest produce, you could organize a community event promoting local farmers and sustainable agriculture. Not only does this make you stand out as a business that's actively supporting local communities and sustainability, it's also a newsworthy event local media would be keen to cover. The key here is authenticity. Your actions must align with your brand's identity, mission, and values. When you undertake initiatives that resonate with what your brand stands for, it not only makes a great PR story but also strengthens your brand's reputation.

I should clarify that doing something doesn't always mean grand gestures or expensive campaigns. It can be as simple as a restaurant sourcing its ingredients from local producers and promoting the farm-to-table concept, a bookstore hosting author meetups and reading sessions, or a tech startup developing an innovative solution for a local problem. It's about doing something that adds value, creates a positive impact, and showcases your brand's uniqueness.

Once you've done something noteworthy, leverage it. Reach out to local newspapers, magazines, and TV stations. But don't stop at traditional media—consider digital platforms like social media, blogs, podcasts, and industry-specific online publications. Don't shy away from sharing your story; remember the essence of PR is communication.

However, doing something worth talking about is only half the battle won. Your PR efforts should be strategic, target the right audiences, and be communicated effectively. Develop a compelling narrative around your initiative explaining why it's important, what impact it has, and how it reflects your brand's commitment. Your story should engage, inspire, and resonate with your audience.

Remember in the world of PR, it's not just about who screams the loudest—even though it might seem that way sometimes. It's about who has the most interesting and authentic story to tell. So, as a small business owner, focus on creating a story worth sharing because PR comes easier once you have done something.

Don't wait for the news to come to you. Create it. Do something that aligns with your brand, adds value to your customers, and makes a positive impact. Because when your business becomes the story, getting the right PR becomes a lot easier.

46

RED OCEAN STRATEGIES: THERE IS BLOOD IN THE WATER

James's Unvarnished Take

I've always been the type of person who if I smelled blood in the water, I thought it was time to eat, not to escape. There was so much emphasis over the years on blue ocean strategies. I think we all understand that because as tech has boomed, it's certainly created a hell of a lot of billionaires. The thing is, it's still easier to look at an existing business and find ways to improve it or modernize it, and still make tens if not hundreds of millions of dollars.

From the 2000 tech boom to the crazy post-COVID stock market extravaganza, we still get starstruck about starting the next unicorn. That's a mistake for most people as the likelihood of starting the next billion-dollar startup is low. It is far more likely to go into a business that's been around for a long time where if you just improved it, you would also become very wealthy. This is essentially what I call red ocean strategies. Highly competitive, well-established markets are in need of modernization, and it's all for the taking.

Technically, that's how I made most of my wealth. I did start off in the tech world as a teenager, but I moved on to more traditional businesses that were just lacking strategy and forward thinking. You can drive up and down any street right now and find inspiration. Much like how a new restaurant takes out an old restaurant, this can apply to almost any business.

Many people out there have been around for thirty or forty years and they haven't adapted. They have products and services that society needs and AI won't replace, solid businesses. Many lack a digital strategy or even any kind of social media or media in general strategy. Many have given up on trying to expand because they're already wealthy. For some people, it gets to the point where they're not willing to work that fifty or sixty or seventy hours a week anymore. They want to spend time with their grandkids.

These are all opportunities to seek out a traditional business and use growth strategies to outwork them. In our ideal world, you purchase one of these legacy companies and bring in the new way of thinking and try to grow them by 200–300 percent. Imagine exiting the business for two to three times what you bought it for because you came in with a modern-day strategy. Just saying that right now gets me excited, and I'm not even the one involved. Anytime you can make a crazy amount of return on your money, you should get excited. Now you're focused on an exit where one day you, too, can just go worry about hanging out with your grandkids.

You must get out of that old way of thinking that everything that was before us isn't worth it and only the new things matter. Unfortunately, that's where the tech world has brought us. If it's old, it's bad, and if it's new, it's good. I'm not sure everyone agrees with that. You must mix the best of both worlds.

Some may ask what are some of those businesses? The list is endless. The world needs window cleaners, landscapers, CPAs, and housecleaners, all things related to building and maintaining a home. The list also includes personal training, fitness and wellness, career coaching and guidance, carpet cleaning, dog groomers and pet resorts, rental properties, music, couches, restaurants and chefs, transportation companies, babysitting, and personal assistance It's endless. Find one, go hard, and never relent. The competition is tired, so don't stop until you have it all.

Kane's Methodical View

In business strategy metaphors, there are two seas: the blue ocean and the red ocean. Blue ocean strategy, coined by W. Chan Kim and Renée Mauborgne, speaks to the creation of new, uncontested market space where competition is irrelevant. Technology is a lot like this; think of the large social media platforms and what their competitive space looked like when they first entered the market. However, not every entrepreneur has the luxury or the means to navigate the tranquil blue waters of limited competition. Sometimes, we have to dive into the red ocean—established markets where fierce competition turns the water bloody.

Red ocean strategies involve competing within existing industries, trying to outperform rivals in order to gain a greater share of existing demand. It might seem like a daunting proposition to throw oneself into a crowded, competitive, and possibly stagnating market. Yet there are countless success stories of companies that have done just that, turning red oceans into seas of opportunity.

One notable example is the rise of Dollar Shave Club. The men's grooming industry was, by all accounts, a red ocean dominated by a few major players such as Gillette and Schick, that had controlled the market for decades. When Dollar Shave Club entered the scene in 2011, it wasn't creating a new market or product. Razors were nothing new. What was new was the approach.

Dollar Shave Club seized an opportunity within this red ocean, providing a subscription-based service that delivered quality razors right to the consumer's doorstep. It rejuvenated a stale legacy industry with fresh, creative marketing, convenience, and affordability. The company grew rapidly and was acquired by Unilever for a reported $1 billion just five years after its launch. Their success lay not in creating a new market, but in seeing and exploiting opportunities in an existing one.

Succeeding in a red ocean requires a different approach. Businesses must develop a strong value proposition, something unique and compelling. Dollar Shave Club did this with the introduction of a subscription model in an old, stuffy space. In a saturated market, consumers already have options and a new entrant must give them a compelling reason to switch. This must be achieved through innovative product features, superior customer service, lower prices, or a unique business model.

Next, entrepreneurs must grind away and chip into market share. It's about recognizing patterns, questioning industry norms, and looking for fresh perspectives. Dollar Shave Club's subscription model disrupted the industry because it challenged the traditional way razors were sold and marketed. Then Dollar Shave Club marketed the hell out of its product such that you couldn't ignore it.

Finally, successful red ocean strategies often involve building strong relationships with customers. As competition revolves around capturing existing demand, understanding customer needs, preferences, and behaviors is critical. By fostering customer loyalty, businesses can maintain a competitive edge even in crowded markets.

So, while blue ocean strategies are attractive for their promise of uncontested market space, red ocean strategies represent a vast sea of opportunities for businesses willing to dive in. It requires courage, innovation, and persistence, but as companies like Dollar Shave Club have shown, it is possible to turn bloody waters into seas of profitability and success. As an entrepreneur, don't shy away from the red ocean—instead, see it as a challenge to bring new life and perspective to established markets.

47
SOCIAL ISN'T FOR EVERYONE

Kane's Reflective Thoughts

There's a myth in digital marketing that every business, regardless of size, industry, or customer base, should be on social media. Yes, social media has its benefits: it's a fantastic platform for increasing visibility, engaging with customers, and promoting your brand. But here's the key—social isn't for everyone. Not every business will find the same level of success or even relevance in the social media realm.

Let's take a look at B2B businesses, those that operate in industries such as manufacturing, logistics, or industrials. These industries often deal with complex processes, niche markets, and specific audience groups. In many cases, they do not sell directly to consumers, their products or services aren't necessarily aspirational, and the buying cycle is typically more elongated and considered than in B2C. The dynamism and instantaneous nature of social media platforms like Instagram or TikTok might not lend themselves as naturally to these industries as they would for, say, a fashion retailer or a food delivery app.

This is not to say B2B companies can't or shouldn't use social media. LinkedIn, for example, has proven itself an effective platform for B2B marketing, fostering professional connections, and facilitating industry discussions. However, it's important to understand the nature of these platforms and the audiences they attract. Posting a picture of a new industrial manufacturing machine might not generate the same kind of engagement on Instagram as a trendy new pair of shoes would.

Social media marketing, like all marketing, should be about return on investment. It requires time, resources, and strategic planning. If you're running a small business with limited resources, it's crucial to ask: is the time and money you're investing in social media giving you the returns you need? If your target audience isn't actively engaging with your content or if the leads you're generating are negligible, it may be time to reassess your strategy.

Instead of trying to be present everywhere, choose your platforms wisely. Perhaps your resources are better invested in search engine optimization, email marketing, or industry-specific digital publications. Remember marketing success isn't about following the crowd, but understanding your own unique context and aligning your efforts accordingly.

Another consideration is the quality of engagement. Social media platforms are about interaction, and it's crucial to have the capacity to respond to comments, messages, and reviews promptly and appropriately. If your business doesn't have the bandwidth for this, a neglected or poorly managed social media account could do more harm than good to your brand reputation.

Remember there's no one-size-fits-all approach to marketing. Social media, while powerful, is just one piece of the puzzle. A successful marketing strategy is a mix of different channels and tactics tailored to your business needs, industry context, and target audience.

While social media has become a dominant force in today's marketing landscape, it's not mandatory for every business. Recognize your business's unique position and don't let the noise of the crowd drown out your judgment. Just because it seems like the latest and greatest thing, doesn't mean it has to work for your small business. Focus on what truly drives value and growth for your business, whether that's social or not.

James's Dogged Analysis

Looking back ten years, I really want my money back. Okay, so that's partially true when it comes to ad money spent on social media. We learned over the years that social isn't for everyone when it comes to generating sales. Many influencers pushed social media; they published a couple of books making you believe everyone can get rich if they use it. And what you found out is social media works well for some types of companies and not so much for others.

Probably one of the greatest lessons we learned in the past decade is that social media as a revenue driver in the business-to-business space has a much lower ROI than business-to-consumer companies. If you're an influencer trying to build a personal brand or if you're a local food truck, or, hell, someone as big as Chipotle, social media is a valuable tool. It certainly works better in the B2C market than in the B2B space.

A lot of times now, we talk about monolithic marketing. It's one of the practices at Daggerfinn. When you think of monolithic marketing, it's the idea that everything the world can see serves to generate new sales but to also attract new talent. Often when we're working with a B2B company, we start to look at their social media more for driving in new talent and employer branding rather than just trying to drive in new business.

When we're doing growth consulting, we start looking at the ROI. If you spent $100,000 on Facebook and Twitter ads, what would it possibly net you? Then we look at if you spent the same $100,000 on AdWords, what could it yield? What if you took the $100,000 and hired a salesperson to pound the phone for 255 business days a year instead?

More times than not you'll find out the $100,000 was better spent in other ways than pushing ads on social media, especially if your business sells to other businesses. Now some people in the B2B space have figured out ways for it to work, but the truth is nine out of ten companies, when you talk to them about the ROI of their social media, can't give you the number. They usually say things like "we do it because we have to." We say if you don't have numbers to prove it, you shouldn't do it.

As social media has matured and you add how much noise there is, the value is beginning to diminish. In some cases for B2B markets, if you want to be on social media, you look at something like LinkedIn. You might be able to squeeze some ROI out if you do the right LinkedIn campaign, for example. It's easy to get caught up in this idea of being instafamous or having 500,000 Twitter followers.

When we do sales process engineering, one of the things we like to measure is yield. For every dollar spent, how many people are we getting into the funnel and how much revenue does that generate? Again, in the B2C market, you can run ads. Someone jumps on your website, they order a product, and it ships. It's a piece of cake. In the B2B world, sales are often more complex; the sales cycle might extend out three to six months and it doesn't work in the same way as selling sheets or luggage.

So social media can work for many different types of companies, but it certainly isn't for everyone when it comes to generating top-line revenue. One of the strongest values of social media for all companies is the employer branding aspect. If you can't use it to generate sales, then keep in mind that before someone joins your company, they're going to look at your social media. This is a great opportunity to show what a cool and fun place it is to work.

Whatever content you write or whatever photos you post, keep in mind current or new customers might see these along with your current and future employees. This is how you squeeze maximum value from social media regardless of what kind of company you are.

48

THINGS THAT
SELL THEMSELVES

James's Unswerving Opinion

One of my first couple of gigs in the tech world—I was probably nineteen or twenty years old—was for a manufacturing company. I was young and didn't know much about business or the world, so I had to listen a lot and soak it all up.

Now, in the Detroit area and in manufacturing, back then there was a high chance you were surrounded by automotive enthusiasts. People often complained the big three were being run by "the bean counters." It was a time when you would come across newly minted MBAs who would say you could run a company just by the numbers. Maybe you can, but we'll save that debate for another day.

Now, depending on who was in the room, that argument would take shape, usually numbers versus design. The car enthusiasts would say that when the engineers run the company, they design cars people want to buy. And when you design a car people want to buy, you don't have to run commercials or spend money on advertising. That car driving down the road is an endorsement in and of itself.

So let's start thinking about all these products you don't see commercials for. I don't remember seeing a Starbucks commercial. You don't see other brands, from Chanel or Hermes to Chick-fil-a, running ads, at least around here. Most likely they run none at all. Just thinking about Chanel, it seems like several times a year they do price hikes and there's still a line out the door. Come on! What a wonderful position that must be in terms of brand equity.

There are so many benefits when products sell themselves. You don't have to spend the time and money to develop and manage a sales team, for example. In the case of cars, you don't have to spend a tremendous amount of money on ultra-creative commercials plus the ad spend for the viewers. If you're not spending all that money on ads and a sales team, think about how much more cushy your margin is. Another way to look at it is that all that money saved can be spent on product development.

We often talk about operating where the air is thinner. We try to do things other people can't or are not willing to do. We like to compete in spaces where the price is higher and the margin is greater while having less competition. But that takes a mindset of not trying to compete on price or trying to thrive at the bottom. One thing you learn in business is that many people start off as sucker fish leeching around the bottom, trying to find any little scraps they can get. It's crowded down there. It's easier, but not always the most profitable.

It should be a goal to get your company or brand into a place where you don't have to justify the price. I'm guessing when Chanel goes through price increases, they don't have to sit there and justify the why. It must be nice to just say the price is the price. And if you don't like that price, there's five people in line behind you who don't mind it. Yes, it is hard to build high-end luxury brands from scratch, otherwise everyone would do it, but there are lessons here.

In a world where everyone seems to take the easy way out and they want to compete on price, does it not make sense to go the other way? There is room in the middle. Many people don't want the best product or the worst product. They want the middle product that is going to do everything they need it to do. You likely still have a decent margin here, but you are going to have to have a compelling story or sales team because you're going to be fighting the companies who have the lower price. And not just them because you also have companies above you that have a better product or the perception of a better product. If you're going to do all that, why not compete at the higher end?

When you have the reputation, things will often sell themselves. Whether it's the hype of the best chicken sandwich from a drive-through window or a timeless classic like Rolex where you can see passing the timepiece down to your children, it's easier when people come to you.

The lesson here is, never stop innovating and keep working on your product or service until it sells itself. We, as entrepreneurs, often rush things to market or get inflated ideas in our head of how great our invention is. You can't stop there. You must keep making improvements until your product or service starts to get people excited.

You keep working on that recipe until people are craving it two or three times a week. If you're creating a product, you must make something that makes other people jealous when they see someone else with it. And if you're delivering a service, you must make that service so valuable the customer cannot fathom not having you at their fingertips.

The other solution is managing a massive sales team, often with high turnover and spending a tremendous amount of money on ads. All of these are margin killers on top of it. So of course you can go the easy route and compete with a lower quality and price. But in the end, it may be better to be the car company that allowed engineers to design cool shit that ends up selling itself.

Kane's Analytical Take

The goal for any entrepreneur should be to create something so profoundly useful, so perfectly tuned to customers' needs that it practically sells itself. These are the products that draw a "Duh, of course I need that" reaction from customers. They address real needs so effectively that people wonder how they ever managed without them.

You might think this thing that sells itself is an elusive unicorn, the product of happenstance or genius. I'm here to tell you it's not. It's the product of an unglamorous but vital process entrepreneurs know all too well: iteration. Now, why is iteration the key to creating products that sell themselves? It's because iteration is all about learning. When we put our products into the world, we are conducting a giant experiment. We're testing our assumptions about what people need and how best to meet those needs. Iteration means taking what we learn from each round of this experiment and applying it to the next version of our product. It's a way to tune our offerings to our customers' needs, making them more compelling with each iteration.

Iteration also enables the creation of products that sell themselves because, in an interesting way, the process builds trust. Each new version of a product is a promise to customers that we're listening to them and working hard to meet their needs. As we deliver on these promises with each iteration, our customers grow to trust us more. They know we have their best interests at heart, and they're more likely to buy from us as a result.

However, while iterating on the product is critical, it's also important to understand the best marketing can't make up for a mediocre product. Yes, excellent marketing can get your product in front of customers and might even convince them to make that initial purchase. But if your product doesn't live up to the hype, they won't come back.

In contrast, excellent products breed customer loyalty. When customers love what you sell, they don't buy just once. They come back again and again. They recommend your product to their friends and family. They write glowing reviews. They become not just customers, but fans.

But how do we know when we have a truly excellent product? How do we know when it's time to stop iterating and start scaling? Here's the truth: iteration never truly stops. Even when your product is selling well, there's always room for improvement, always another customer need to address, another opportunity to increase value. The key is to keep iterating, but also to recognize when you've reached a point where your product is indeed excellent. When your customers are delighted, when they're advocating for your product, and when they're coming back for more, that's when you know you've got something special.

Remember the goal of all this isn't just to make money, although that's a nice side effect. The goal is to create something that truly makes people's lives better, something that addresses real, pressing needs so effectively people can't help but say, "Duh, of course I need that."

That's the power of a product that sells itself. It's not just a product. It's a solution. It's a promise kept. It's the embodiment of your company's values and mission. And yes, it's the result of countless iterations and a whole lot of perseverance. Don't aim for good. Don't even aim for great. Aim for excellence. Aim for that "Duh, of course I need that" reaction. Iterate until you get there. Then keep iterating. That's the path to a product that sells itself and a business that stands the test of time.

49

CUSTOMER LAZINESS & PROCESS SIMPLIFICATION

James's Unyielding Perspective

Thinking back to when I started my first business and how difficult it was to get a simple contract together sure brings back memories. Like anything, when you start a business, you must do all of these fun things like get together scopes of work, contracts, and payment terms. You go to your lawyer and say you need a contract. They come back in a couple of weeks and give you a twelve-page document only another attorney could decipher. Then you say, "Look, man, if I send this to them, it's going to go right in the trash can. Can we do something simpler?" Their answer usually is no unless you push back. It's one thing to legally protect yourself; it's doing good business. It's a whole other thing to make it so complicated no one ever wants to do business with you. There is a balance in there somewhere.

After chipping away at the lawyer for several more weeks, we came up with a much shorter agreement that was down to about two pages. In an ideal world, I wanted one page, but this wasn't too bad and clients were more willing to sign it and return it quickly.

Mark Cuban put out a book that was essentially a culmination of all of his blog posts. Somewhere in there he mentioned the same thing about making it easy for your customers to do business with you. Every time I'm on a website with a checkout that makes me fill out a tremendous amount of unnecessary information, it rings in my head that these people have not thought about making this any easier. There's been many times when I just closed the window because I am annoyed or irritated as it keeps asking for the same damn information over and over again. Or you didn't fill a box out so it resets the form and you have to start over. Okay, peace out, I am taking my business elsewhere.

That's the cool part about Apple Pay and other similar payment options. Instead of filling my address out three different times—one for the billing address, one for the shipping address and another one for the online account—I'm just going to double tap this button and go about my day. These payment options allow the consumer to do business very easily. Not only does it make it very easy, when you look at the data about how many items are left in shopping carts that never convert to sales, you have to wonder whether people were rethinking the purchase or if it was just too damn complicated to check out.

I can think of many times I bought something just because it was that easy to do it. I'm sure if I would have spent another five or ten minutes thinking about it, I probably would have talked myself out of it. But no, with the Apple Pay buttons there, click-click-boom, more stuff coming to the door and I can't even remember what the hell it was I ordered.

Just being a consumer every day, if you're paying attention, you can get a lot of inspiration of how to make it easy for your customers to do business with you. This may be having a poor experience yourself or even a good experience. Right now, a poor experience that keeps ringing in my head is trying to order off one of the delivery apps for food. Many of them don't give you the option to modify things.

Maybe I don't like onions and mushrooms, so give me the damn option to remove them. They don't give you the checkboxes and they don't give you a note section. So now I just choose not to order from them. Or, if I want it bad enough, I have to place the order and then turn around and call them to say, "Hey, can you remove all this stuff?" More often than not, I choose to go to a different restaurant, and human behavior says that's probably what happens most of the time anyway.

As someone who is invested in the restaurant industry, I understand why you don't want that note box, though. When you put the note box there for people to make modifications to their food, the likelihood of the people in the back of the house making a mistake goes up dramatically. This is a common problem in the business world. We know what the consumer wants, yet we choose not to do it because we can't execute it properly. Putting systems in place and training people to pay attention to their notes would resolve most of these issues and you wouldn't be losing customers anymore.

People are busy these days. Tolerance for waiting is shrinking by the minute. We're no longer patient. You add all of that up with the fact that there's an endless amount of competition and choices and you see the problem clearly. If you're not making it easy for your customers to do business with you, they just go somewhere else.

This is why Amazon succeeded in such great fashion. It was one of the first big players to hit the market with a system in place that made it so easy to order you would order things you didn't even need. When I'm in the office and someone tells me, "Hey, we need pens, paper, some coffee pods, and some paper towels," in less than a minute, before they walk out of my office, I've already ordered it. I'm not joking. In less than a minute, this was all done.

They have your billing address, your shipping address, and your payment and everything's already uploaded and ready to go. Shipping options? No problem. You have Prime; it's coming tomorrow. They have all of the products you need in one place with a simple shopping cart and a simple order button. Click-click-boom, task is done. On to the next one.

You must look for ways to make it that easy for your customers to do business with you. I'm talking a lot about payment options because that's where conversions tend to fall off. Things that often slow you down are complex contracts, annoying payment terms, or lack of payment options. Also, the more people you have to get involved to make the decision and to sign off on things, the more it slows everything down. If you have a contract a department manager can sign off on because it's easy, it's far more likely it will get signed because it doesn't have to go off to legal review, for example.

In the past twelve months, we had to turn a vendor down because their payment options were so damn annoying. Everyone else on the planet, if you're using a monthly service, will allow you to throw a credit card in and let it auto bill. This was a rather large company. It had no reason to not have a payment processing option on the back end. It's time to close the deal. We're looking at the contract, and the only option is to pay by check or wire. We're like, "Look, you have no option for me just to throw in the American Express and let this thing auto bill every month?" They didn't have it and they didn't even want to find out a way to do it even though today it's extremely easy to do with technology.

Well, it's time to look for a new vendor then. If you're trying to take somebody's money, you should make it as easy as possible for them to get you their money. But still today, businesses refuse to adapt and make things easier for the consumer. We all have a certain level of tolerance of what we think we should have to do as part of the process. No one ever questions if it's too easy, but people will begin to question things if they are too complicated.

The lesson of the story is, if you send your customer a two-page contract instead of a twelve-page contract, there's probably a higher chance they're going to sign. If your customer wants to pay you with an American Express card, let them pay you with an American Express card. If they want to order your food online, allow them to make whatever changes they want. Hell, charge for the changes to the food. Just make it easy for me to get what I want.

Never underestimate how lazy someone can be when it comes to parting with their money. They are willing to spend it, but they're not willing to jump through silly hoops so you can take their hard-earned cash.

Kane's Reasoned Analysis

Marketers often focus on the quality of the product or service they offer, the effectiveness of their strategy, or the brilliance of their marketing campaign. One aspect that often goes unnoticed, however, is the "laziness" of the customer.

To a business owner, the idea of lazy customers might sound negative, even offensive. After all, we often prefer to imagine our customers as active, engaged, and eager to embrace our product or service. However, what we call laziness is simply human nature. People are time-sensitive, tend to take the path of least resistance, and are often reluctant to change their habits. Harnessing this knowledge is key to creating an environment that encourages purchases and enhances customer satisfaction.

Consider the meteoric rise of Amazon. One of the secrets to Amazon's success is its focus on reducing customer effort to the barest minimum. It introduced features like one-click purchasing and automatic replenishment of everyday items, and streamlined returns to an art form. Amazon effectively anticipated and navigated around customer laziness to create a user experience so frictionless shopping elsewhere seems arduous.

Being aware of customer laziness and proactively working around it requires an intimate understanding of your product and its interaction with the customer. Are there steps in the purchasing process that seem cumbersome or unnecessary? Can the product setup or usage be simplified? Is there a way to make reordering or renewing more straightforward?

Take Dollar Shave Club again for an example. It is a subscription-based personal grooming company. Instead of expecting customers to remember to buy new razors, Dollar Save Club delivers them regularly to the customer's doorstep. This ingenious strategy leans into customer laziness by removing the need to repeatedly purchase.

Your digital presence is another area where accommodating customer laziness can pay dividends. A slow-loading website, a confusing interface, or a convoluted checkout process can quickly deter an online shopper. Streamlining your online experience to make it as easy and quick as possible can help capture those customers who would otherwise abandon their cart.

The same principles apply to brick-and-mortar stores. IKEA, for instance, made the shopping experience so straightforward customers can almost navigate their stores blindfolded. The flow from room setups to flat-pack furniture to checkout is so smooth it makes shopping, traditionally viewed as a chore, akin to an enjoyable experience.

In customer service, businesses can leverage the understanding of customer laziness by making help readily accessible. A customer who runs into an issue with your product or service is more likely to abandon it than to spend time searching for a solution. Immediate, easy-to-access customer service can be the difference between retaining a customer or losing them.

The goal is not to breed further laziness, but to empathize with the customer's desire for convenience and simplicity. This perspective fosters an environment that respects the customer's time and energy and promotes an atmosphere of ease.

Embracing the concept of customer laziness is a potent strategy for any business. By anticipating points of friction and proactively simplifying the customer's journey, you not only increase the likelihood of initial purchases but also foster an environment that encourages repeat business and customer loyalty. After all, in a world that seems to be spinning faster each day, who can blame a customer for wanting things to be just a bit easier?

50

MARKET SHARE: IT'S TIME TO HOARD

James's Unrelenting Insight

On *Shark Tank*, one of the things that always pisses the sharks off is the concept that "this market is so large that even if we just take 1 percent of it, we can make millions." From a business perspective, you understand why the sharks feel that way as there's no guarantee that's how it will work. On the other hand, at several of our own companies, we had the same mentality, and we have gone on to create several multimillion-dollar companies from scratch. This is essentially harvesting enough breadcrumbs to make a meal. Interesting enough, the largest business in that group, we did that while the market for that business was shrinking.

One quick side note before we continue. What I think the sharks miss sometimes about this concept is real demand. The last thing you want to do is to have to educate a consumer about a product or service they never knew existed. It's expensive and your customer acquisition is extremely high. It's much easier sometimes to go into a market where you know there's already a tremendous amount of demand. Think about it. If you're about to run an online campaign in a search engine, how would you do that for something people aren't even searching for? So sometimes it is nice to know you're jumping into a market where people are already spending billions of dollars.

Back to our regularly scheduled episode. This particular business focused on manufacturing companies. Technically, you can call it any and all things industrial \ manufacturing and supply chain. When manufacturing was shrinking by GDP and the service sector was continuing to grow, we decided to keep our foot on the pedal and keep trying to get as much manufacturing business as possible. When we told other people that, they couldn't process why we would continue to chase a shrinking market. We were thinking the whole time, "Why wouldn't you chase this market?"

We doubled down on the manufacturing sector and became experts in that field. Sure, the market was shrinking, but our share of that market was rapidly increasing. As everyone else chased fads or whatever sector was booming at that moment, we hunkered down and carved out our name as a specialist in that sector. See, we weren't just gathering breadcrumbs; we were getting whole slices of bread.

It's one thing if the market is completely dying. Maybe it's not the best idea to double down on going after that market. If you think about it, though, if you keep trying to sell regular landline rotary phones as mobile phones are coming out, your balance sheet is probably not looking so good right now.

In another chapter, we talked about how everyone chases blue ocean strategies because new markets are where billionaires are made. The problem is, the barrier to entry is extremely high and it's not built for the average Joe to get in and play that game. The great thing about red ocean strategies, in our opinion, is that many of these businesses have been around for a long time and just about anyone can jump into them. Maybe some of those markets are shrinking, but many of them are still begging for improvement.

The thing about a shrinking market is your competitors tend to take their focus off of it. We say let them go jump on the new fad or whatever industry. Our name will still ring out in ten years as the experts in this field because we never gave up. As your competitors focus on other industries, you simply have less competition.

Just think about this for a moment. If the industry is going to shrink by 10 percent in ten years but 50 percent of your competitors are going to chase other markets, can you not see where your opportunity is actually larger now even though the market is shrinking? That's how we ran the math. Yeah, the market was shrinking a little bit as the services sector and technology grew, but we found it easier to get customers because of the lack of competition.

Even better yet, as we experience a manufacturing renaissance in all of its renditions plus the current push to onshore manufacturing again, we're sitting in the best spot in the world. We have built up so much brand equity it's not likely anyone else will catch up.

It takes intense focus to hammer down on one sector and keep grinding away until everyone knows your name. This was much easier to do because the market shrinking made the competition leave.

What you typically see in the modern business world is what we call "shiny thing strategy." It's that meme you see online where someone's like "oh, shiny new things" as they bounce around distracted by anything new presented to them. Many modern-day business operators struggle to focus. They see someone succeeding somewhere else and they think, "Hey, why not just go jump in over there?" And when that doesn't work out, they see someone succeeding in something else and they go jump in over there. What they didn't realize in the beginning is, all that jumping is exhausting.

If you have the perseverance to keep grinding while staying focused on the market that fits you best, it will eventually pay off. You can't fall for the shiny new things trap. It would be the equivalent of us focusing on the manufacturing sector and then jumping into tech for a little while and then when mortgages boomed jumped into that market—well, you get the point. You're no longer a specialist. You're just someone riding the waves and eventually you'll come crashing down.

Opportunity is endless. It may shrink, gently retract, or aggressively expand, but it's always there. It's like that old saying about "when preparation meets opportunity." Problem is, you're never prepared if you're chasing something new every twenty-four months.

Let's close this one out. If the market is not going away anytime soon and it's something you can dominate, then it seems like your best bet is to double down on what you do best.

Kane's Measured Perspective

An adage in business says, "Elephants don't swat flies." In other words, the big players often overlook the small fries. In fact, it's why large companies are always at risk of being disrupted—because when bureaucracy comes into the frame, things really slow down. For small business owners, this is a golden opportunity, especially when it comes to capturing market share in a large market.

First, let's understand what market share means. In simplest terms, it's the percentage of the total sales in a market captured by a business. In larger markets, where the pie is extensive, even a small slice can translate into substantial profits. Small businesses can often feel intimidated by the thought of venturing into markets dominated by industry giants. They see the huge revenues, widespread recognition, and robust resources of these titans and think, "How can I possibly compete?"

But this mindset is where many small businesses falter. Instead of cowering in the shadow of industry titans, smart small business owners see an opportunity to shine. The reality is, the bigger the market, the more niches there are to exploit, the more customers there are to serve, and the more room there is to grow.

So how can a small business compete and win its share in a large market? First, it's important to understand you don't have to reinvent the wheel or come up with an entirely unique product to compete in a large market. What you need is differentiation. By offering something different—be it superior quality, innovative design, exceptional customer service, or more attractive pricing—you can stand out and attract customers.

The beauty product industry provides an excellent example. Despite being dominated by giants like L'Oréal and Estée Lauder, there has been an explosion of small, independent beauty brands in recent years. These companies didn't introduce a new type of product; they differentiated themselves by offering vegan, cruelty-free, or all-natural alternatives and by connecting with customers through social media and influencer marketing. These small brands may capture only a tiny fraction of the multibillion-dollar beauty industry, but their share is still incredibly lucrative.

Second, agility is a small business's best friend in a large market. While industry giants are like huge ships that take a long time to change course, small businesses can be speedboats, able to adapt quickly to changing trends and customer needs. This agility allows them to stay relevant and seize opportunities faster than larger competitors.

Consider the case of small craft breweries. Despite the dominance of brewing behemoths like Anheuser-Busch and Heineken, craft breweries have carved out a growing share in the beer market. Their secret? Agility. They can quickly adapt to changing consumer tastes, introducing new and creative brews the giants can't match for speed and originality.

Finally, remember capturing market share is not just about having the best product or service. It's about making sure your potential customers know you exist and understand why your offering is worth their attention. That's where marketing comes in. By leveraging digital marketing channels—from social media to SEO to email marketing—small businesses can reach a wide audience and grab their share of the market.

The online eyewear company Warby Parker is a prime example. It entered a market dominated by Luxottica, a giant that owns brands like Ray-Ban and Oakley. By offering stylish glasses at lower prices and implementing a direct-to-consumer model, Warby Parker caught consumers' attention. And with clever marketing campaigns, it continued to grow its market share.

So, while it might be daunting to step into a large market, don't let the size of your competitors scare you off. Remember even a small piece of a large pie can be satisfyingly substantial. It's not about outdoing the giants at their own game but about playing your own game better. With differentiation, agility, and strategic marketing, even the smallest businesses can carve out their lucrative slice of the market.

51

TAKE OVER YOUR BLOCK BEFORE YOU TAKE OVER A NATION

Kane's Structured Viewpoint

You've heard it before: "Think global, act local." But when starting a business, a more accurate mantra might be "Start local, then go global." Your neighborhood, your block, your city—they are not just where you live; they are your first and most accessible markets.

The rationale behind this is straightforward: proximity breeds familiarity, and familiarity breeds understanding. You know the people, the culture, the infrastructure, the gaps, and the opportunities because you are a part of that community. It's your home ground, and there is no better place to start.

Let's consider the example of Howard Schultz, the former CEO of Starbucks. Before Starbucks became the global giant it is today, it was a single store in Pike Place Market in Seattle. Schultz understood his local market—Seattle's thriving coffee culture—and tailored his product accordingly. He offered high-quality, freshly brewed coffee as an alternative to instant coffee, which was popular at the time. The local market embraced it, laying the foundation for what Starbucks is today.

This doesn't mean you should limit your vision to the local market. It simply means focusing on your local market can provide a strong starting point from which you can expand. This is especially true in industries like food and beverages, retail, and services, where the local market's preferences can significantly influence your product or service. In-N-Out Burger, a popular fast-food chain in the American West, began as a single store in Baldwin Park, California. The brand's understanding of local tastes and preferences, paired with a focus on quality and service, led to a cult-like following. They have successfully expanded across multiple states, but their roots remain in their local market.

Taking over your block also allows for a more straightforward feedback loop. Your customers are not faceless entities hidden behind screens; they are people you see and interact with regularly. You can talk to them, observe their behaviors, understand their needs and wants, and use this information to adapt and improve your offering. The more you understand your customers, the better equipped you are to serve them.

For instance, the founders of Nextdoor, a social networking service for neighborhoods, leveraged their local knowledge to build an online platform that addresses community-specific needs. They launched in a single neighborhood in San Francisco. By focusing on local communities, they gained a deep understanding of user behavior, allowing them to refine and improve their platform before expanding it to neighborhoods across the United States and then the world.

Once you've made your mark locally, you can replicate your success in other markets. The insights you gain from your local market will inform your approach to new markets, albeit with necessary adjustments for cultural and demographic differences.

Conquering your local market—your block—can provide a solid foundation for future growth. The knowledge and insights you gain are invaluable, offering a deeper understanding of your customers and a blueprint for scaling your operations. As you strive for global success, don't overlook the power of local. After all, the world is nothing but a collection of local markets.

James's Aggressive Approach

Sometimes, we have to consume content in order to get inspiration or ideas. You can go for a drive and listen to music or maybe do a little people watching. Travel works pretty well or even just reading the book. For some reason, when I think about strategy, I like watching shows like *Billions* or *The Wire*. Now *The Wire* is my favorite show of all time and many other people agree. There are so many business lessons in that show I could write a whole separate book just on that. While the neighborhood I grew up in wasn't nearly as crazy as Baltimore, it did remind me in a way of where I grew up and the time I spent hanging out in southwest Detroit.

One of the things that show always gets me thinking about is dominating your territory. Funnily enough, as Stringer Bell became more business savvy, he wanted to get away from fighting for territory. Fighting for territory also meant dropping bodies, which is going to bring heat from the police. On the other hand, Avon Barksdale didn't want to back down and lose his corners. That was his territory he had fought hard for over the years and he didn't want to give it up to a competitor.

Every day in the drug game, people fight over just a corner. That one corner alone could be worth a tremendous amount of money, especially if it's the right corner. Those corners are worth going to war over. While you're fighting locally for those corners, it's also such a small territory you're not fighting with people from twenty miles away.

We use this example because when you start a business or you're developing a growth strategy, as entrepreneurs, we always have this grandioso idea of going after the entire market. We've all made that mistake when starting a business. You must sit back and ask yourself, "Why am I trying to win a client in Texas when there are one hundred companies within twenty minutes of my local office I could do business with?"

In a way, every business has its own corner it needs to fight over. It's probably a good idea to dominate your local market, whether that's a city or county or at most a state before you try to take over a whole country. If you're trying to compete on a national level, you're certainly going to find a hell of a lot more competitors.

For several of our own businesses, when we looked around to see who the local competition was, we found out there was none. When we cold-called locally, we found out no one had cold-called them in over a year. There's no competition or sales pressure from the local market. Here we are right down the street where we can meet this prospect at their office or for lunch. How ideal is that?

Now if we went after Chicago, there would have been a lot more competition. At that time, we didn't have a Chicago office or a sales team yet. Why would we target Chicago when we would have had a tremendous amount of local competition that could walk down and meet them in their office or have lunch with them? Or we would have to explain how our team in Michigan could help them in another state. It ends up making a hell of a lot of sense to focus on local first and dominate that market before you expand outward.

If Stringer and Avon tried to take over one corner here and another corner five miles away and another corner three miles away from that and another corner ten miles away from that, do you think they would have become the kingpins they were? It's possible as not much was going to stop these guys, but it was likely significantly easier to take over a bunch of the best corners in one little area of the city. For supply chain reasons to muscle, having everybody in one area was more efficient and way more effective.

When you have an office with your team and you're focusing on servicing local clients, it just makes too much sense. Companies are also more willing to work with a business that is local. When we would cold-call out of state, we still would have a lot of success based on our reputation. But our close ratio wasn't nearly as high as what we had in our own state.

For just about any business out there, there's millions if not tens of millions of dollars of business just in your state alone. When you think about that, why go after a whole nation when you haven't even taken over one corner down the block? The goal should be to take over your local block first and then figure out a plan for taking over the block on the next street over. You do that until you build up a critical mass and a brand equity to where it makes sense to attack other markets outside your local one. Once you reach a point of saturation, it's time to look at other places that have a lower amount of sales pressure so you can go there and apply your own.

Once you get in that mentality of this is my territory and I'll do anything to defend it, it's not likely anyone is going to come in and take it from you. We often design multi-brand strategies to put extra pressure on markets, so it's even more difficult for competitors to squeeze in. This is why I love the idea of owning your local street corners. You muscle up and put enough pressure on that market to where no one else can squeeze in. As noted before, it's significantly harder to do this five or six states away, but maybe you'll get there one day.

Knowing there's a tremendous amount of business right down the street from you, it wouldn't make sense to not go get that first and worry about everything else later. Dominate your local market and keep fighting for that territory until no one else is willing to fight for it. Once you've done that, it's time to take over another block.

I'll close with one thing you have to learn only once: it's a hell of a lot cheaper to keep the clients you have than it is to go out and try to find new ones.

52

DON'T WASTE COPIOUS AMOUNTS OF TIME ON THE FUN STUFF

James's Uncompromising Insight

Oh, the memories of starting your first business. You think you're so clever. You just think you're one keen mickey fickey. You have all of these ideas, slogans, and a logo, and the creative juices are flowing like the bottomless rosé fountain we used to get at Katana in Chicago. Funny enough, when I got back to Chicago, that place was actually out of business. But it was one hell of a happy hour to take the Chicago crew out to for a warm-up.

Over the years, we've created more than a dozen brands and invested in countless others. Every year, you get a little smarter and the things you thought mattered so much no longer do. You become more efficient and you realize what it really takes to get the business off the ground and moving. To keep it simple, you need a product or service ready to be sold. When I look back and think about how much time we spent arguing about business names, logos, and mission statements, I often wish I could get those hours back.

Whether you're rebranding an existing business or creating a new one, things like your logo and your mission statement have significant meaning. But at the same time, as a group of consultants often focused on yield and effectiveness, there comes a point when you're just spinning your wheels.

We love to get things right, and it's great if you can get them right the first time, but that's likely not possible. I'm not sure who said this, but if you have 70 percent of what you need, it's time to go. This is a difference between being meticulous when it comes to your branding and thinking the company name or logo needs to be. The reality is, it's rarely the primary reason someone chooses to do business with you.

The funny thing is, the first big client I ever landed barely remembered my name let alone my company's name, nor had they seen my logo or mission statement. What I was telling them on the phone was a service that would directly meet their current needs and solve their problem. They said okay, let's go.

There was probably about a $25,000 check we earned, and the gentleman on the other end of the phone didn't care about how long we were in business or what we were trying to achieve. He didn't ask who our current customers were, nor did he want a reference. He was paying for an outcome and it was that simple. He felt, based on our conversations, that we could deliver the outcome he needed.

We probably have one hundred domain names in a stash and another fifty LLCs sitting on standby for all of these ideas. Some of them will never be utilized and some we will work on diligently until they become fully realized. We will spend a small amount of time getting logos and mission statements together. We like our brands to feel cohesive, to be modern, and to explain exactly what it is that we do without saying it. But at the same time, we're not looking to spend ninety days to figure that out. We're going to look to get that done as efficiently as we can and then start selling the product or service.

You run into people who filed a ten-dollar DBA with the county with some made-up silly name like Acme 123. They spent money on AdWords or they picked up the phone and started war dialing, or as we said back in the day, dialing for dollars. They had a product or service that someone wanted to buy, and they kept up the marketing and selling until someone bought it. It sounds crazy, but it really is that simple. Spending money and time on marketing and sales, you'll never look back and feel like you didn't get a reasonable ROI on that.

That's why we often say to limit the time you spend on logos, mission statements, and tomfoolery. People spend so much time trying to make the perfect business card even though most people throw it away after you hand it to them.

If you're going to spend that much time worrying about a business card, try spending that time working on your website with a content strategy and SEO plan. You don't hand out business cards anymore; you connect with somebody on LinkedIn. No one cares about your mission statement. I'm not even sure in my twenty years of doing business across multiple sectors, if anyone has actually asked me what my mission statement is. Even if they asked me, I'd probably be like I'm here to sell you shit and take your money. How much more transparent can I be? You'll need a good one, just not right now when you're employee one of one.

Your biggest problem along the way is probably going to be hiring the talent you need to grow your business. Instead of working on mission statements, maybe work on a manifesto or EVP. Most companies don't even have an EVP or understand what it is. It's an employee value proposition. To put it in another way, it's a small paragraph explaining why in the hell you should work here in the first place. That's the funny thing about growth strategies and trying to scale the business. It's not your logos, your business card, and your mission statement that gets you there. It's the people you're surrounded by, the ones who show up with the hard work and creativity that make the things happen. Then you grow.

When you're a management consultant you're always trying to solve X: Why this? Why that? This wasn't happening, now it is, so let's do a regression analysis and try to figure out where everything went wrong. Nine times out of ten, where it went wrong is, you probably hired the wrong people. Almost all problems can be solved with the right people. Most problems are caused by hiring or not firing the wrong people. By the time you got to this chapter, you can see that's a reoccurring theme throughout this book. Your talent pool and workforce culture are everything.

The logo didn't land the deal for you. Your sales executive did, or your digital marketing strategy brought in the lead organically. The mission statement wasn't some intrinsic motivator that made everyone work together as a team to make things happen. Instead, you likely hired the right people who had the mindset to come in and make great things happen all while sharing a common goal with everyone else in the company.

I think back to the days of the excitement of designing your first business card with your logo and coming up with clever taglines that you believe at the time, if someone reads it, they're automatically going to sign your contract. The memories of going to Staples to buy pens, paper, and letter organizers because you're about to get so much mail still give me goosebumps. It's similar to when you build a house and you find yourself at Home Depot often. Nothing smells better than the fresh wood in Home Depot.

Then reality sets in. Everything smells good and you have a cart full of wood. But someone still has to build that house. That's when you reset the priorities and put an emphasis on the things that really matter. The lesson here is, spend more time building the house than walking around Home Depot. You'll never regret the time you spend trying to acquire customers and sell your product and service. If you want to scale or get something off the ground, you have to build. But nothing's going to get built until you start swinging that hammer.

Kane's Pragmatic Approach

In the race to set up a successful business, entrepreneurs often find themselves tangled in the web of creating the perfect brand identity. This might involve devising the perfect business slogan, designing an eye-catching logo, building a sleek website, or distributing visually striking name cards. While these elements are undoubtedly important and contribute to a company's overall image and appeal, they can sometimes turn into a tempting distraction, pulling the focus away from what truly matters: turning the proverbial "open" sign on and welcoming your first customer.

Imagine spending countless hours perfecting your company slogan—a catchy, clever string of words that encapsulate your brand's mission, values, and promise to your customers. You go through rounds of brainstorming, bouncing ideas off friends and colleagues and refining each word until it perfectly embodies your brand. You do the same for your logo, website, and other branding elements, pouring time, energy, and perhaps a significant portion of your budget into these endeavors.

But amidst this whirlwind of creative brainstorming and refining, the clock is ticking, and the world outside your brainstorming bubble is spinning. Every day spent fine-tuning your slogan or website design is a day not spent on your actual product or service, a day not spent engaging with potential customers, a day not spent driving your business forward.

In the business world, time is the most precious commodity, and in the realm of startups, it's even more critical. This is why it's imperative to act fast and execute. A perfect slogan on a closed door is far less impactful than an average one on a door that's open and inviting customers in.

Consider this: the most memorable slogans we know today didn't become iconic overnight. They grew in significance and impact as the companies behind them delivered on their promises. It was the consistent quality of the products, the effective service delivery, and the overall customer experience that gave life and meaning to those slogans. Without the delivery of tangible value, even the most cleverly crafted slogan would be empty.

The same can be said about logos, websites, and name cards. These are important components of your business's image, but they're merely the vessel for your brand. They carry your brand to your customers, but they can't create the substance of your brand. That comes from what you deliver—your products, your services, your interactions with customers.

None of this is to say that slogans and other branding elements are unimportant. Instead, it's a reminder that they are just one part of the broader business ecosystem and should not be allowed to overshadow the more substantive aspects of your business. Strive for a balance that allows you to establish a strong brand identity without losing sight of your primary goal—to do business, to create value, to serve customers.

In the early stages of your business, it's essential to maintain a lean and agile approach, focusing on activities that bring you closer to launching your products or services and earning your first revenues. Once you have started to establish a customer base and steady revenue stream, you can afford to spend more time refining your branding and other elements.

Remember starting a business is not a beauty contest—it's a race against time, competition, and resources. It's a journey filled with challenges and obstacles that require decisive action and quick adaptation. The sooner you can turn on that "open" sign and welcome your first customer, the sooner you can start learning, adapting, and growing. So put on your running shoes, act fast, execute, and let the journey begin.

53

EXPERIMENT WITH MARKETING

James's Thoughtful Reflections

Working in the creative space can be one of the greatest things you ever do and at the same time one of the most infuriating things you ever do. It's not finite like mathematics, where there's only one right answer or it can be done only one way. When you factor in trying to understand the concept a client has in their head and then trying to get the creative to bring that concept to life, it certainly can create some difficult days. At other times, when you nail that idea and you have the whole room looking at you like how the hell did you come up with that, it's one of those highest high feelings that you never want to stop.

The hardest thing here is understanding you have to keep trying things until you find something that works. As business owners doing in-house marketing, we're looking for that kill shot. We want to find that one thing that works every single time that allows us to recoup our marketing investment, that helps grow our top line without wasting much money. And what you learn after decades of building companies is that it's just not feasible and you have to let go of that way of thinking.

Often it goes like this. You have the most clever idea in the world where everyone around you is like "wow." Then that concept falls flat on its face. You can't sit back and say you're not going to spend any more money on this because you had one failure. Because while you're doing that, your competitors are out there working on new campaigns until they figure out something that works. And once they figure out something that works, they're going to be out there taking your customers and your market share.

Whether you're in the C-Suite of a large company or an entrepreneur, you understand it is irritating as no one wants to waste the money and time to find out. But that's creative work. There is no nail in the coffin on this one. Sometimes things work and other times they don't, but you can't be afraid to stop trying.

Some of my best examples come from the time I spent working in the music industry recently. I'm producing an album for a friend, and we're often locked in the studio for ten to twelve hours or more at a time. We're trying different things on the beat, we're going back and forth writing different lines to see what flows better. Eight of those ten hours might be trial and error. What sounded good in theory didn't sound so good on the mic. One crazy idea we had ended up sounding amazing to the point where it's like, okay, now we have a hit. You just can't pop into the studio and lay this thing down in an hour and expect the whole world to think it's going to be a banger. Sometimes one day is not enough. I know Grammy nominated multi-platinum artists that sometimes have spent twenty-four hours or more locked in the studio trying to get one verse right. But that's why they're Grammy nominated and multi-platinum. They kept grinding away until they got it right and they never gave up.

Not only do you need experience with the creative, but you also need to figure out what platforms are going to yield you the best return. It doesn't matter how much you read online and try to get your answer, there's only one way to find out and that's to go do it. In another chapter, we talked about how social media doesn't seem to work that great for business-to-business sales. It's not that it can't work. It's just that the time and money might be better spent somewhere else that will get you a higher yield.

You may find certain social platforms work better than others. Maybe you have some deadly combination of Facebook and Twitter or Instagram and TikTok. Each platform has its own pluses and minuses, especially when it comes to how detailed you can get on demographics.

Now you also have to find out whether still photos or videos work better for you. Are you better off just posting clever tweets and promoting that to your core audience? If you're on TikTok, maybe you avoid going the insightful route and try to do something funny. Let's not forget about LinkedIn, which is often a greatly overlooked platform, especially for B2B companies. It's a good place to do insightful content or to give someone a downloadable asset so you can get people into your sales funnel.

Let's step away for digital for a moment. Even for some of our own businesses, we still run traditional TV commercials, depending on the type of business. We'll get a higher ROI and yield more customers through traditional media sometimes more than just digital. Have you ever thought about putting a booth up at an industry conference? What about starting your own podcast and spending marketing to get more views for that podcast? You can experiment with marketing in many different ways.

Radio listenership is down, but people still listen to the radio. One of the coolest things I remember was with a radio show that was on Saturday mornings in Detroit. I believe they were mortgage guys or finance guys, and they would take over the radio station for a whole hour. For that entire hour, all they would talk about was mortgages. People called in and they answered their questions. Talk about building brand equity and generating sales all at the same damn time. There are other ways to do that today through a podcast or even starting a series on YouTube. That could be audio only or, if you want to get more sophisticated, create a video and film it.

There are people out there running single-camera-only operations who have built large channels that have generated a metric ton of money. For our next video project, we're probably going to use three cameras, two fixed and one on a slider. Do we know if that's going to work? Not sure yet, but that's our vision and we're going to give it a try.

Sooner or later, you'll find that thing that just works. Once you find that thing that works, you can scale it. And you're going to run that thing until you run it into the ground and then you're going to go back to the drawing board and try to figure out what the new thing is.

In an ideal world, you don't wait for your original campaign to end. You want to have the next thing already locked and loaded, fully tested and ready to go. The lesson here is you can't be afraid to try new things. Don't be afraid to blurt out your idea. If it gets shot down, it gets shot down. You can't let insecurity ruin the creative process. Even worse than that, don't be the person who has this idea in their head and they're afraid to say it, and then someone else says it and gets the credit for it.

If you're signing off on these budgets, you can't be afraid to spend the money. You don't have to overspend, but it's going to cost some money to find out. Set your risk tolerance and then grip and rip.

Unless you're lucky enough to have a product that sells itself, you have to keep pushing the creative and find new ways to drive sales. Just keep in mind that if you're not doing this, your competitors are, and you can't be surprised if you get left in the dust.

Kane's Strategic Perspective

I'm in the mood to talk stocks and the financial markets for this chapter, so let's light this candle. Marketing strategy can often feel like investing in the stock market. Like the dizzying array of potential investments, a multitude of marketing channels vie for your attention. And just as good investors diversify their portfolio to maximize returns and mitigate risks, smart entrepreneurs spread their marketing efforts across various channels to ensure maximum reach and impact.

Just like investing, marketing begins with understanding your target demographic. A seasoned investor studies market trends, company profiles, and economic indicators before deciding where to put their money. Similarly, an effective marketing strategy starts with detailed customer personas—knowing who your customers are, where they spend their time, and how they like to communicate. This knowledge guides where to invest your marketing efforts.

Next comes the choice of channels. Just as a financial advisor would advise you not to put all your money in one stock, it is crucial to spread your marketing investments over different channels. Each channel, be it social media, SEO, email marketing, or content marketing, has a unique reach and appeals to a different segment of your target demographic. Some might prefer catching up on Facebook, while others might prefer skimming through informative blogs. By diversifying your marketing portfolio, you ensure you reach all segments of your target audience.

Setting clear goals for each marketing channel is as essential as having a financial goal for your investments. Just as an investor may invest in a specific stock to gain a particular percentage return, set specific, measurable objectives for each channel, defining what success looks like. It's the equivalent of tracking the performance of your stocks, analyzing trends, and making informed decisions for future investments.

The story of Glossier, the cult beauty brand, is an excellent example of this strategy. Glossier recognized the habits and preferences of its customer base and leveraged Instagram to appeal to their love for aesthetics and digital community. Then Glossier continued to diversify its marketing investments. It tried pop-up stores, email marketing, and user meetups, effectively diversifying its marketing portfolio and increasing its reach.

Running these marketing experiments can feel like monitoring the performance of your investments. With time and data, you will see some channels performing well, while others might not meet your expectations. This information is invaluable. It allows you to refine your strategy, invest more in high-performing channels, and divest from those that underperform.

Embracing marketing experimentation is akin to becoming a savvy investor. It's about not putting all your eggs in one basket but spreading your risk across a range of options. It's about taking calculated risks, learning from the market's response, and constantly tweaking your strategy based on data and results. It's about recognizing that not all investments will pay off, but those that do can yield significant dividends. In the world of business, the key to successful marketing is not about betting everything on a single card, but playing a well-thought-out hand.

54

DON'T CREATE SOLUTIONS TO PROBLEMS THAT DON'T EXIST

Kane's Careful Consideration

Like a scene out of the movie *Wall-E*, the business world is littered with the scraps of products meant to solve problems that didn't exist. These are products that, while perhaps innovative or interesting in their own right, were simply not needed. They were answers in search of a question, solutions seeking a problem.

For entrepreneurs and marketers, it's easy to fall into the trap of creating a solution and then seeking a problem it can solve. However, this approach is fundamentally flawed and more often than not leads to failure. In fact, achieving a successful product-market fit is challenging enough when you're addressing a real, widely recognized problem. When you're trying to address a problem that doesn't exist, it's nearly impossible.

You see, the key to achieving product-market fit lies in understanding your market, its needs, and the problems it's facing. Then and only then should you design a product to meet those needs and solve those problems. The best products and services come from companies that have intimately understood the pain points of their customers and have worked tirelessly to offer a solution.

So before you start building your product or service, ask yourself, "Is this a problem that needs solving?" Is this something that keeps your target audience up at night? Is your solution something they would pay for? If the answer is no, then perhaps it's time to revisit the drawing board. Remember a great product or service is not just something that's well designed or technologically advanced. It solves a real problem or fills a genuine need for its users. It addresses pain points, makes life easier, or offers a unique experience or benefit users can't get elsewhere.

Your focus should always be on the user, the customer, the human being at the other end of the transaction. Don't fall in love with your solution—fall in love with the problem. The more intimately you understand the problem, the more capable you are of creating a solution that truly addresses it. Sure, innovation and creativity are vital in entrepreneurship and marketing, but they should always be grounded in the reality of your market. Don't waste your resources—time, money, and energy—on solutions looking for problems. Instead, spend those resources understanding your market, its needs, its pain points. From this understanding, create solutions that address these needs and alleviate these pain points.

A key part of understanding your market is understanding your competition. What solutions are they offering? How can you do it better? Here's where innovation comes in—not in creating solutions for nonexistent problems, but in offering better, more effective, or more efficient solutions to real, existing problems. In fact, looking at the competitive landscape is a great way to assess the viability of your idea. To the work and research extensively first.

Don't create solutions for problems that don't exist. It's a trap that's easy to fall into, but ultimately it's a pathway to failure. Instead, focus on understanding your market and its problems, then create solutions for those problems. That's the pathway to success, to a product or service that's not only innovative but also truly needed—and that's the kind of product or service that has the best chance of achieving a successful product-market fit.

James's Unabashed Reflections

Driving down the road recently, I heard a news segment on CNBC or maybe it was Bloomberg. They all sound the same. They were talking about the Microsoft CFO saying on a conference call something like "don't go build a golden toilet" to people of Microsoft. It was funny because that seems like what the tech industry thrives on, building things people don't need and haven't asked for. The best part is, no one wants to pay for it. I'll take that back. Post-COVID, it's pretty crazy what people were willing to spend their money on. When the printing presses were cracked open, we watched financial discipline go out the window. Fortunes were made and lost in that two-year period.

The past couple of decades have taught us a thing or two, though. As we built our group of companies, we also looked at investing in others over the years. We get pitched all the time and sometimes the pitches are completely wild. One thing in common though, with many of them, is that they created solutions for problems that don't exist. The founders were so enamored with the idea being so cool or that no one has done this that they had blinders on. You try to tell them, "Hey, man, no one has done this before and it's probably for a good reason."

It's hard to pick the winners and losers, though, we get that. You have to bet someone told the slap chop inventor it was a silly idea. Next thing you know, half of TikTok is slap chopping away as they make viral garlic bread. We all have drawers and cabinets of things we thought were cool but never use. So sure, it's possible to be a quick buck artist with a fad product; we are just trying to aim a little higher with our strategies.

During the tech boom, these types of companies would raise some money and go bust. If they were lucky, they would spin the company and IP off for a few bucks and then they would go build another golden toilet, this time with diamonds on it! The new and improved diamond dump 2.0! Funnily enough, they'll get funded again too...

The good news is, though, the world is full of problems that need to be solved. If not problems, the world is full of inefficiencies that waste our time and money. Not every innovation has to be revolutionary. Sometimes even incremental improvement of a product or service is enough to invigorate your consumers.

We get lost in blue ocean strategies because that is where the big money is made. But at the same time, ignoring the things in front of you just begging for its next rendition could also be costing you billions. Before you start a business, expand your product line, or bring up that new service idea in the board meeting, do this one thing first. Ask yourself, "Does this really solve a current problem?" If not, you better know how to create the problem, too, so you can actually sell what it is you're creating.

OUTRO

Congratulations, you've reached the end of this journey. As you've navigated through the pages of this book, you've likely revisited familiar knowledge, discovered new perspectives, and, ideally, been inspired to implement positive changes in your department or organization.

Consider a line from the movie *The Social Network*, where the character of Mark Zuckerberg remarked, "Fashion is never finished." It's an insightful thought. Fashion continually evolves, with trends rising and falling, old styles reviving, and innovative ideas breaking ground. Much like fashion, your business is never truly finished.

From enhancing company culture to boosting productivity, to refining employer branding strategies to exploring new markets for sales, there will always be facets of your business that are in perpetual development. The landscape is always shifting and what worked one year may falter the next. As you strive to grow your company, you'll launch various marketing campaigns. Some will succeed, some won't, but the learning never stops. Even a booming sales period will plateau eventually. The key lies in agility, adaptability, and hunger for the next big thing.

Business has never been more competitive. If you're not perpetually striving for improvement in your business, organization, or function across culture, operations, and beyond, rest assured there's a competitor who is ready and eager to seize the advantage.

Consider this book your blueprint. Read a chapter a week, then ask your team how the insights can be harnessed to drive incremental improvements in how you do things, day after day. Real change doesn't occur overnight—it demands persistent efforts over months, even years, to create lasting improvements.

In today's business world, passivity seldom breeds success. If you desire something, you have to strive for it. In a world as competitive as the one we live in nowadays, now is not the time for meekness, but for innovation, for audacity, for relentless pursuit of excellence. After all, we're competing not just locally or regionally. There are global players vying for the same business that is our lifeline, our livelihoods.

The saying goes, "you never get what you don't ask for." If you're waiting for a handout, allow us to save you the time—it's not coming. Instead, rise to the challenge, demonstrate resolve, cultivate an unyielding improvement mindset, and, most important, never settle for less. Settling is the path to disappointment. Remember, it's not just about the destination, but also the journey. To the moon we go.

INDEX

Made in the USA
Monee, IL
17 June 2024

59547851R00184